TEACHER TO **TEACHER** Publications

Inquiry Teaching in the Sciences

BARRY J. FOX, TERRI GROSSO and PHYLLIS TASHLIK

ANN COOK: SERIES EDITOR

TEACHERS COLLEGE PRESS

COMMUNITY STUDIES, INC

Grateful acknowledgement to the Bill and Melinda Gates Foundation and Community Studies, Inc. for support provided

Distributed by Teachers College Press, 1234 Amsterdam Avenue, New York, NY 10027

ISBN 0-8077-4565-0

Manufactured in the United States of America

11 10 09 08 07 06 05 04   8 7 6 5 4 3 2 1

CONTENTS

PREFACE

Scientists inquire. They challenge themselves with difficult questions, make careful observations, develop hypotheses and test them, search for evidence, analyze results.

Good science teaching, when based on inquiry, develops the very same skills for students.

This booklet introduces the reader to inquiry teaching in the sciences. Two perspectives have been included. Part I, based on a group of teachers participating in a summer workshop, follows their experiences as they become the students in an inquiry-based science workshop. Part II illustrates how an entire science course for high school students might be developed using the inquiry approach.

Both the teacher workshop and the student course have been used successfully in the small schools of the NY Performance Standards Consortium.

PART
I

TEACHERS AS STUDENTS: LEARNING THE INQUIRY APPROACH

BARRY J. FOX • TERRI GROSSO • PHYLLIS TASHLIK

Teachers who have participated in inquiry workshops respond:

"An inquiry teacher's role is to have students observe and question as much as possible. At the same time, students use the scientific method to pursue answers to questions."

C. W., Coalition for Social Change, NYC

"The role of the inquiry teacher is to help students use their experience to observe and discover. The teacher is the facilitator of education as opposed to the giver of information. . . . Inquiry realizes that students come to us with ideas and knowledge; the inquiry teacher allows them to use what they know to find out the answers to problems. When students prove something for themselves, they are better able to retain information than if they simply received it from a teacher or textbook."

B.R., Vanguard High School, NYC

"Participating in inquiry activities has confirmed my sense that being an inquiry student can be fun."

S.R., Institute for Collaborative Education, NYC

Introduction

As part of the performance assessment system developed and practiced by small schools, teachers are expected to engage students in inquiry learning and hands-on experiments in their science classes.

Part I of this booklet is based on the experiences of a group of teachers participating in a week-long summer workshop on inquiry-based teaching in the sciences. The teachers were placed in the role of students, not just teachers, of science. They began at the beginning: with observations and questions. From there they re-experienced the discovery of the scientific method as a means for solving problems.

This booklet will give you an idea of the thinking behind the inquiry approach to teaching science and help you develop your own ideas for designing hands-on experiments for your students. Several suggestions are explained as the narrative follows the teachers through three experiments—one each in biology, chemistry, and physics—and touches on their discussions about pedagogical concerns. To illustrate how accessible inquiry teaching could be, the activities and experiments mostly grew out of the usual "cookbook recipes" found in traditional science texts. The teachers then discovered, as one of the teachers noted, "that I can actually create my own inquiry lessons all the time" by building on what is easily available.

We hope the description of this workshop inspires you to trust your students' curiosity, their need to know and find out, and their capacity to internalize, not just memorize, the steps in the scientific method.

The Scientific Method

HORTICULTURE EXPERIMENT

Active learning in science begins with questions and hands-on experience. Day one, and the group leader immediately asked the teachers a basic question for any introductory science class:

Under what conditions do string beans germinate best?

As part of the inquiry approach to teaching and learning, they were then asked to probe further and consider which questions the question itself raised. Just as students do in inquiry classrooms when asked, the teachers arrived at many questions, which the group leader wrote on the board:

What types of conditions should be considered?
How long does germination take?
What does "best" mean?
How should data be gathered?
What will we need to find out?
What specific type of string bean is used?
Where does it normally grow?
What does "germinate" mean?
How much individual variation is there?

The teachers quickly saw that each question raised further questions. For example, when they focused on the conditions needed for germination, they pursued these:

How much watering is needed? How often?

How much light?

What type of medium is needed? What type of soil? Will any soil do?

Is fertilizer needed?

What is the best way of planting? How deep in the soil should the seed be placed?

What is the best data: Height of the stem? Percentage of total number of seeds that germinate? Would two healthy plants be better than seven sickly plants?

For students, the above questions could lead to a continuous series of experiments that might last weeks, even months, with students introducing different variables and learning the skills of observing, researching, data collecting, analyzing, note taking, lab report writing. The attraction of this experiment is that while the seeds are growing, the class can explore other areas of experimentation and research.

But for their brief time together, the teachers began their inquiry with a conversation about the definition of "germination." Even there, more possibilities arose: Is germination signaled by the first appearance of growth above the soil or below? Is germination the very first sighting of growth, regardless of where it occurs? If so, are special containers needed—ones with glass fronts so that the growth could be observed *below* the soil's surface?

These questions stimulated others in the group to rethink what had at first appeared to be an obvious definition. As teachers formulated more and more complex responses, one suggestion was offered to test seeds for starch at varying intervals to know when they were just about to sprout (seeds contain less starch and more sugar as they approach germination).

SMALL GROUPS

At this point, the teachers were broken into smaller groups to design their experiments. Their instructions offered no more direction than to ask each group to respond to the initial question: *Under what conditions do string beans germinate best?* Each group had to decide which definition they would use for germination, which conditions they deemed necessary for carrying out their experiment, and what their hypothesis would be.

Working in small groups opened up the conversation, encouraged the quieter members of the group to speak, and allowed different approaches to flourish. And, as happens with students, the teachers began to question each other more in their effort to understand each other's ideas and suggestions. As a result, as one teacher noted later, the group members "understood *all* the steps the group took," whereas in more traditional approaches to group work in the lab participants often do not understand the necessity for each step that is taken.

Group 1

For the first experiment, this group thought they ought to try thinking as they assumed their students would think (they later realized that, in fact, they *were* students in this setting). They hypothesized that four media were possible for germination: air, soil, water, or a combination of soil and water. As a control for each of these media, temperature and light would be constant. Their hypothesis was that a combination of soil and water would work best. They planted ten seeds and agreed to consider germination as the point when the plant breaks through the seed coat. This decision obviated the need to test seeds for starch prior to sprouting. They also decided to remove the seeds on the fifth day, estimating that at that point they would have germinated.

Group 2

A second group concentrated on the effect of water on germination. They questioned the volume of water that would be necessary to support germination and the quality of the water. Although students might not consider the variations of water available to them, the teachers were able to raise this question for consideration. For watering, they used four different amounts: 5ml., 50 ml., 100 ml., and no water at all.

They also debated the location for the plants, whether indoors or outdoors, on the windowsill. Safety became an issue, and they opted for the indoors.

Group 3

This group became immersed in a discussion about the pH and the way it affects germination. They hypothesized that the pH of the soil would indeed affect germination, but they were not certain how.

Measuring for pH dominated the group's focus and expanded their consideration of the chemistry of the experiment. Is the pH of soil the same as the pH of water? How do you measure the pH of soil? Is the pH of the water used sufficient information?

At this point they referred to horticulture books that were made available to them for research and found that the best pH range for soil was 4 -7. They decided to add acetic acid to the water and vary the dilution for each plant. Someone from another group was able to help them with the logarithms they needed to calculate the math for the dilutions. They settled on four variations of dilution: pH of 4, 5, 6, and one with no acid at all.

Because of the intricacies of their conversation, this group fell behind the others when it was time to set up their experiment. For the teachers, this raised pedagogical questions: What do I do with my own students when this happens? Is it appropriate to permit students' questions to take them far afield of the original scope of the experiment? At what point, if any, should a teacher intervene and reset the line of questioning?

MATERIALS

Basic Materials Needed

seeds for string beans
soil
containers
water supply

Other Suggested Materials

In inquiry, as students develop their own ideas and experiments, they may request materials that take you by surprise.

The materials used always depend on what questions the students ask. For this experiment, you can probably anticipate the following:

Which is the best media? Have available different potting soils, perlite, vermiculite, and peat.

Which is the best size of container? Have available a variety of sizes.

What temperature? Provide access to a refrigerator and possibly an incubator.

Different amounts of light? Provide access to a dark area, different kinds of bulbs and light timers.

It's always fair to say, "We don't have that. Can you think of some other way?"

Intervention

The groups' experiences described above provide an excellent example of the types of pedagogical issues that arise with any hands-on experiment. Suppose, for example, students were not providing enough water for their plants to survive. Should the teacher intervene to correct the mistake before the plants die and the experiment fails? How much information should a teacher give a student? *Can* an experiment fail, or does each experiment in its own way provide useful information?

The teachers debated their thoughts about intervention. They were concerned about students who might feel frustrated by experiments that flopped—that their frustration might be more powerful than their curiosity. The group leader pointed out that feeling frustrated or discouraged with an experiment is simply part of what every scientist goes through. As proof, the group leader mentioned that by the second week of classes, it's a good idea to invite a guest speaker to meet with students and answer questions about his or her own research and the challenges of being a scientist. Inviting guest speakers into the classroom is a powerful technique for introducing students to the field of science. Speakers should be cautioned in advance, however, that their role is not to lecture but to answer questions about their work and research.

The teachers seemed to reach a balance concerning intervention. They agreed that if the main purpose of an experiment would not be compromised, then teachers should be able to intervene in students' work. If, however, intervening would compromise the purpose of the experiment, then the teacher should refrain from intervening, as difficult as that may be.

It is interesting to note that as the week unfolded and as they participated in additional experiments, the teachers began to understand at a deeper level the importance of being more patient with students, intervening less, and questioning more. As they continued to function as students of the inquiry method, they observed themselves as learners and the ways in which inquiry fostered their curiosity and built confidence.

The inquiry and performance assessment approach to science is markedly different from the approach of the NYS Regents exam. The labs included in the exam assume there is one outcome and are unconcerned about students who don't reach the expected outcome. In inquiry, however, as in the real science lab, an unexpected outcome can be the creative spark for the next experiment.

Timing

What happens in the classroom when the groups function at different paces? In the framework of inquiry teaching, it is possible to have a backup activity for students to participate in.

One practical solution is to have students begin writing their lab reports. This, however, poses additional problems for the teacher since students don't initially understand the importance of writing down data. A suggested assignment for introducing data collection appears in Chapter 2.

FINDINGS

Five days turned out to be insufficient time for the groups to detect germination above the soil; however, when the soil was emptied from the pots, the teachers discovered that many of the seeds had indeed germinated, that is, first growth had broken through the outer covering of the seed. Group 1 discovered that soil and water had provided the best medium and was the medium that saw growth (water or air or soil alone was not sufficient). Group 2 found the best results ("best," for these groups, meant the largest number of plants that germinated) with 5ml of daily watering. The other volumes of water yielded no growth. Group 3 didn't notice any growth at all during the week-long period. Clearly, one week wasn't sufficient to see the experiment through to the end.

An important question the groups never got to was the choice of potting soil. In fact, each group had chosen to use a soil-less potting mixture, probably because it was the largest, most apparent container on the cart. At the time, no one thought about how that might affect results, and it wasn't factored into the conversation (though students often find the choice of soil an interesting question for their own experiments).

Most importantly, teachers discovered that the desire to see growth in a plant was a strong motivator, and although they had been skeptical about what students could do with such an experiment, they later appreciated the possibilities it opened up to them for inquiry. The lesson offers multiple opportunities for learning basic skills embedded in the scientific method: data gathering, research, observation, analysis, lab report writing. For example, even with the limited results obtained after five days, the teachers raised interesting questions concerning data analysis: Should they measure the length of root growth? Should they quantify the number of plants that germinated?

FOLLOW UP

Usually, once teachers have been introduced to inquiry, they enjoy going through the experiments themselves but wind up asking, What do I do next? This group's experience in horticulture shows how the next step grows out of the first. For example, any of the early questions about growth and propagation could initiate an entire series of experiments on growing conditions: soils and other growing media, fertilizers, seed type, climate, and so on. And even if the plants never grew, the next question to investigate would be, why not? Or, why didn't more seeds germinate? Or, which seeds would grow under the same conditions?

Once students have planted a seed, they are motivated to see their plants grow. First they become nurturers—parents of the plants—and then they become scientists.

2 Assignment: Data Collection

How do we get kids to be serious about data collection?

Again, the teachers became students and were asked to go through the experience of collecting data. They were given the assignment below, which has been a successful introduction to data collecting for students.

Count or Measure

This is an exercise in thinking about data collection. Your task is to think of a common observable event that can be converted into numbers. Be as creative, imaginative, and thoughtful as you dare.

You are to count or measure the same event on three successive days and collect data for each day. You will be required to submit your data and a report to the group at the end of the three-day period.

The report must include:

1. A brief explanation of what you counted or measured.
2. Tables and graphs that appropriately illustrate your data.
3. A brief explanation of what the data tell you. What conclusions can you draw? What patterns do you see?
4. A description of any problems that came up as you were collecting your data.

The teachers saw the value of this assignment as they considered suggestions and helped each other develop more complexity in their questioning. For example, one suggestion was to go to Central Park at a specific time and for a specific interval to count sports activities. But during a discussion of the assignment, teachers offered options for making the exercise more complex: Were more men than women participating in the sports? Were ethnic differences obvious? Did gender or ethnic background affect which sport was being played? Who participated in team sports? Who worked out alone?

From Recipe to Inquiry
CHEMISTRY EXPERIMENT

At the end of the previous day, the teachers had been asked to look at one beaker of a clear liquid that contained a penny floating at an angle on the surface. The group was told that at their next meeting they would explore what was causing the penny to float. One of the teachers hypothesized that the liquid could be salt water, which might explain the buoyancy of the penny.

The next day, they were confronted with three beakers: two filled with a clear liquid and a single penny afloat in each and one beaker filled with a blue liquid. All beakers had a dark residue on the bottom.

To answer the question *What is causing the penny to float?* they were told they would have to respond to the following sub-questions:

What is the chemical composition of the penny?
What is the chemical composition of the original liquid?
What is the chemical composition of the blue liquid?
What is the chemical composition of the dark residue?

They were given no other directions, but an array of supplies was made available for their use when requested. Materials were not initially displayed.

Although it is true that, as teachers, they started from a more substantial knowledge base than would their students, they also had a lot to learn about what caused the penny to float. While in their large group, they were asked to explain their working hypotheses. Their responses to their initial observation of the beakers and the above four questions were:

Penny One of the teachers informed the group that pennies are composed of both copper and zinc. (Before 1983 pennies were all copper. After that they were given a zinc core since the copper had become more valuable than a penny.)

Original liquid They hypothesized that the liquid was a concentrated acid since it seemed strong enough to dissolve copper out of zinc (the blue coloring of the third beaker persuaded them of this). They considered measuring its pH value to get more information and because, as one teacher explained, they were "hooked" on solving this problem.

Blue liquid They hypothesized that the blue color was related to the presence of copper.

Dark residue They hypothesized that the residue was dirt possibly left in the beaker from before.

Students would clearly start from a very different point. But the teachers, too, were unsure what they would discover and how to go about discovering it. They asked questions—Is it okay to change the temperature? Can we test the density?—and talked about different ways to get started on their inquiry. Once they were divided into three separate groups, each group went its own way, which in itself is a lesson about inquiry-based teaching and learning in science.

The groups worked steadily for two hours, forgetting even to take their coveted snack break. Their reaction to the puzzle before them exactly mirrored the response of students when confronted with the mysterious floating pennies. They were intrigued. They would later explain their intensity as "fun." It's important to point out that at this point, the role of the teacher in the classroom is to fetch supplies (as the group leader was doing for them) as groups discover their need to experiment, test hypotheses, and observe results. The teacher also circulates among the groups, taking notes and recording how each group is working. These notes prove important later on when the smaller groups report to the full group, since students invariably forget to mention something in their procedure that turns out to be extremely important to the inquiry process. (This actually happened for the teachers as well when one of them overlooked mentioning important details about the penny and the liquid.)

Group 1

The first group immediately began poking the floating penny. They plucked it out of the liquid and noted how easily the exterior copper coating fell away. They quickly saw that the internal core of the penny looked like it was dissolving! Pondering how the core of the penny could dissolve without the exterior going through the same process, they examined the other penny for telltale signs of corrosion. They noticed a nick in its exterior coating. Was it there the previous day when they first saw the floating penny, or had the nick appeared as a result of being immersed in the liquid? One teacher lamented that she had not been a good observer at the beginning of the experiment. She did note, however, that the pennies had all been floating at an angle, "like boats," and that the nicked side had always been up, just at the surface, not below.

They also became intrigued with the dates on the pennies and introduced a 1964 penny and a more recently issued penny into the experiment. They hypothesized that the newer penny, which contained more zinc, would float first. But more importantly, they experienced how an inquiry project can lead participants to explore new questions that had not been anticipated in the original plan for the lesson.

Although they had previously been skeptical about embarking on such an experiment without prior knowledge about the properties of the materials involved, one of the teachers said that all she needed to read in an available text was that "ammonia can be used to identify the presence of copper" to begin getting ideas about the type of exploration she wanted to do. Others felt that a prior knowledge of chemical symbols and equations was first needed to make use of the text. But overall, how difficult would it be for a student to ask a teacher to interpret Cu as copper or Zn as zinc?

Group 2

This research-grounded group began with textbooks. Based on the blue coloration of photographs in a chemistry book, they concluded that the liquid in the beakers was sulfuric acid (a clear, colorless liquid) and the blue color was caused by copper ions. They also focused on density tests of different liquids. Indexes in the texts provided them with the most help for locating the information they needed. (They later learned, during group discussions, that the liquid was not sulfuric acid.)

Group 3

The teachers in this group presumed that the liquid was an acid based on its viscosity. Their first step was to do a pH test, which confirmed that the liquid was an acid; however, the pH didn't tell them which specific acid. One of the teachers was concerned throughout that although they found the liquid could have been hydrochloric acid, the tests didn't confirm that it was hydrochloric acid.

While focusing on the pH, by accident they observed bubbles issuing from a nick on the edge of the penny. Their discovery showed them how, with time, their observations were becoming more detailed—a process that occurs with students as well, provided they're given the time to become increasingly involved in what they're doing.

The observation of the bubbles alerted the group to the chemical reaction taking place in the penny, something they had not noticed earlier. Some sort of displacement was taking place between the metal inside the penny and the acid. Although students may not have the vocabulary of their teachers and would not be able to use the term "displacement," they too, if observant, would become aware of the bubbles and realize that a critical interaction must be taking place between the liquid and the penny.

THE INQUIRY PROCESS

It's interesting to note the different approaches that the three groups took. Group 1 members jumped right in and began putting hands on whatever materials they could, observing small details, like nicks on the edges of the pennies. Group 2 was more cautious and chose to first research what they could in science textbooks they were already familiar with. And Group 3 combined both approaches, sometimes jumping in and sometimes researching in order to test their hypotheses.

But also like the students, the teachers became fascinated by the process that unfolded for them as, step-by-step, they tried to understand why the pennies were floating. As one teacher commented, "The more engrossed you became in the experiment, the more carefully you observed." They also agreed that the dialogue that emerged among them in their groups piqued their interest and engaged them, especially as they began to play with ideas and possible approaches. Some of the teachers felt that initially their background, or lack of background, in chemistry affected their confidence in themselves as problem-solvers. But as the process itself engaged them, they became more deeply invested in understanding exactly what was going on with those pennies.

Findings

As a whole group, the teachers agreed that the liquid was hydrochloric acid, although no one had actually showed it conclusively. They also agreed that the zinc reacted more quickly to the acid than the copper. They never completely agreed on what the residue was.

Experiment leads to experiment

The teachers were so curious by the questions raised during this experiment that Group 1 pursued another experiment to confirm that the zinc alone was responsible for the gas release. Using a new beaker filled with hydrochloric acid, they submerged sections of thin copper wire that appeared to be pure to see what would happen. They also added pure zinc to another beaker. What new information would they learn now that they had established new controls?

PEDAGOGICAL CONCERNS   What did the teachers learn by going through an inquiry process?

In the beginning, for some, the activity had seemed appropriate only as an application or reinforcement of something that students had already learned through a more traditional approach. They were doubtful students could learn new material or even new ways of thinking from the activity. They questioned whether the activity could be given early in a unit on acids or chemical reactions.

As they went through the stages of the experiment, however, they were clearly committed to the work they were doing and highly curious about the results. For example, they came in the following morning and immediately went to the beakers with the pure copper and pure zinc to observe an entirely new chemical reaction: a precipitate had formed in the beaker where the copper wire had been placed. What was it? In the beaker where they had placed the zinc, a black precipitate had formed. What was that? A whole new avenue of inquiry appeared that could not have been anticipated before.

Recipe vs. Inquiry

The original textbook "recipe" for this experiment was distributed to the teachers and the contrast with the inquiry approach they had used was more than apparent (see the Appendix for information on the textbook). In contrast to their experience with the floating penny, the textbook's approach struck them as restrictive and certain to discourage rather than encourage curiosity and ownership.

The teachers agreed that inquiry allowed for individual differences and variations in learning styles while fostering curiosity and a sense of play. But they also appreciated the research aspect of the process and the availability of texts for referencing information they would need. Further, they saw how one experiment can lead to other experiments and other questions that students would be motivated to ask. For example, when students observe the bubbles, they might try to figure out a method for calculating the bubbling rate, which would then help them learn more about the internal properties of the penny, since stronger metals produce a faster release of gas.

Inquiry provided more than "fun"; it yielded hard information:

- two metals, zinc and copper, react differently to hydrochloric acid
- the chemical reaction produces a gas (the bubbles), a solid (the residue), and copper ions
- copper ions cause hydrochloric acid to turn blue
- ammonia can help detect copper ions in the solution

The teachers' experience with inquiry brought home to them the value of having students participate in small groups while conducting hands-on work. The groups helped them overcome the difficulty of getting started on a project and their dialogue and exchange of ideas, hunches, and information were invaluable for solving the problems before them.

FOLLOW UP

Inevitably, after a workshop in the inquiry approach to teaching science, teachers ask, Where would we go from here? At this point, the notes a teacher has kept on the student groups and the full-group discussion become a valuable tool. The teacher reviews the notes and types up for distribution those sections that would be helpful to students.

The notes provide an inquiry summary and serve multiple purposes: they validate for students the work they have done, clarify some of the hard information they have learned, synthesize the concepts they've observed in action, and help students define a new focus for subsequent work. They also provide the beginning of the next day's lesson. (See page 35 for information about the inquiry summary.)

4 Research and Research Design

The group leader presented the teachers with an article that had appeared in the UFT newspaper *New York Teacher* concerning the effects of sugar on children's behavior. The article is a critique of an earlier *New England Journal of Medicine* article that claimed sugar does not affect children's behavior. (See the Appendix for information on this article.) Most of the teachers interviewed for *New York Teacher* claimed they themselves observe changes in children all the time as a result of eating sugar.

The teachers in the workshop were asked to propose a research project that would examine the question *What is the effect of sugar on children's behavior?* They were told that they would work in groups, that each group would then present to the larger group, and that they were all responsible for listening to other groups describe their research model, taking notes, and later asking questions. Each group would develop a hypothesis, an idea of what materials were needed, and an overall experimental design.

As on the previous day, each group found its own approach to the problem. Two groups immediately engaged in dialogue, while the third group began by having each person individually thrash through ideas and take notes before coming together to share.

SMALL GROUPS

Group One

This group selected as their research population a school building that included children from pre-K to 12th grade, thus ensuring a wide age range for their study. By enlisting, on a volunteer basis, 10% of the building's total population, they would have a protocol group of about fifty children ranging in age from four to teens.

Students would be asked to complete a particular task each morning—one that would be easy to accomplish for all those involved, such as building a block tower. Then, at 10 a.m., teachers would provide the volunteers with a standard, small meal with known quantities of sugar and observers would note how much each student ate. The students would then be asked to do the same task a second time.

Observers would note changes in behavior, particularly any aggressive behavior (which they had not yet defined). Obedience would also be observed both before and after the morning snack. Students' teachers, however, would not be made aware of the hypothesis.

The group acknowledged the problems inherent in their design. For example, other children might influence participating children's eating patterns. Also, measuring food consumption could be tricky. And deciding what is sweet or too sweet would be an issue, as well as the choice of food (soda? chocolate?).

Group Two

Group Two's hypothesis was that sugar makes kids more active (but not hyperactive). They proposed a cohort of twenty children and, to ensure that age and gender were not a factor, would recruit two boys and two girls from five different age groups (2, 6, 10, 13, and 17 years old). Before the food program went into effect, they would observe the children's behavior to get a clear picture of their personalities. Then they would alternate "sugar days" and "non-sugar days" during which the children would be fed nutritionally sound and attractively prepared food (a nutritionist and a chef would be used to plan the meals). Because the food would be tasty, the children would not reject the non-sugar foods. Objective observers would be used to record the children's behavior throughout the day, eliminating issues that may arise for "morning people" or "night people"; however, the observers would not know which child was on a "sugar" or "non-sugar" diet for the day. Each observer would have only one child to observe.

When they described their proposal to the larger group, the teachers acknowledged inherent problems. For example, they did not know what they would use to measure children's activity level. They also knew they would have trouble controlling all the meals the children ate during the day.

Group 3

The third group extended their study to seven months so that it would not be limited to one season, and they expanded it to include three school districts across the country. Ten children from each district (for a total of thirty students) would be recruited as volunteers. Incentives, such as money or coupons for sneakers, would be used to attract parents and students to participate.

Students would be observed for one month to detect whether their behavior would be characterized as hyperactive. They sketched out a working definition of hyperactivity: speaking out of turn, getting out of seats, touching others. Also, the children's physical characteristics would be tested throughout each day: blood sugar, pulse rate, etc. One of the three groups of children would continue as before. A second group would receive a snack and lunch with higher levels of sugar. The third group would be split in half: half would remain on their regular diet and half would receive the added-sugar diet. The teachers thought rice pudding would be a good medium for introducing the sugar since it could be tasty and attractive with different levels of sugar content.

Their design would allow for a number of comparisons that could be made between groups, variations from month to month, variations depending on the time of day. Their use of a control would help ensure a more valid comparison.

Questioning

Once each group presented, they began to question each other about their designs. Many of their initial questions focused on methods for obtaining volunteers and consent. Then they gradually turned their attention to variables, controls, and research design. They raised questions about baseline concerns (how do you avoid children who are already hyperactive? how do you get parents to volunteer their children?) and questions about variables (how does a child's weight affect the amount of sugar consumed? how do you measure activity and hyperactivity? what happens if someone sneaks some other foods? how do you account for the subjectivity involved in tasting sweetness?)

Larger questions emerged that could apply to any protocol: What is a valid population? How many should be involved? Would a small group be representative of a large group of children?

By engaging in the design and critique of each other's proposals, students learn the challenge of coming up with a good study and the reality that no experiment is ever going to be perfect. Even scientists have to deal with that truism. They also learn and refine very basic skills in communication. They must listen to each other's presentations, they must take notes, they must ask questions of each other. As a homework assignment, they would analyze their notes and write about each other's strong points and weaknesses.

After critiquing their own research proposals, students would then be asked to read the original article in the *New England Journal of Medicine*. The group leader has done this often with students and has found that by the time students get to the original study, they are capable of critiquing it, analyzing its strengths and weaknesses, comparing it with their own proposals, and sometimes interviewing a scientist familiar with the research.

The teacher's role for this project is, once again, to walk around, listen carefully, take notes about controversies that arise in small group and large group discussions. The teacher's notes are then distributed for everyone to read and to further discuss the controversies that emerge. Students might then be asked to consult other research materials. Have other studies supported these findings? *Does* sugar affect children's behavior?

Medline is a useful resource for students to search for appropriate articles. If a teacher is affiliated with a university, students may be permitted to use the university's library to find articles. Public libraries, of course, can also be useful. Teachers are important during the library excursions, helping students with key words, photo copying, and responding to other basic needs of beginning researchers.

Once students have amassed their research, whole lessons can be devoted to techniques for reading the articles they've found. How do you scan an article? How do you get through something that is boring? How do you get the information you need without reading the whole thing? Contests between groups often help students to focus on some of the details, if not the larger issues: Who's the primary researcher? What is the duration of the experiment? How do you get in touch with the scientists?

From **Recipe to Inquiry**

PHYSICS EXPERIMENT

The earlier chemistry experiment with the pennies grew out of a rather simple science experiment recipe book. Once put through the rigors of an inquiry approach, though, even a basic recipe became intriguing and more representative of real science.

Now it was the teachers' turn to transform a simply presented science lesson into a tantalizing inquiry lesson. In groups, they went through a large collection of science texts and manuals, gleaning them for useful starters (see the Appendix for list of resources). Their interests ranged from microbiology to chemical reactions to physics. They took turns spinning possibilities for each other, trying to see which idea would be most intriguing to work on.

A lot of talk ensued, but also a lot of silence. Silence, perhaps, is the most challenging classroom condition for a teacher. Although we're tempted to interpret silence as disinterest or boredom, silence also indicates thinking. And that's what everyone in the room was doing. The group leader pointed out to the teachers that counting to twenty can be a useful technique before rushing in to fill the silence in a classroom. Most of the time, a student will beat you to it by raising a hand.

The teachers settled upon a question in physics: *Which is heavier, cold air or warm air?* The group that had chosen the question played the role of teacher, helping the other groups develop an inquiry lesson to respond to the question. Their own group would use the recipe experiment provided in the text they had consulted (see Appendix for information on *700 Science Experiments for Everyone,* compiled by UNESCO). The teachers later remarked that it was reassuring to see newer teachers develop an inquiry lesson from a standard textbook recipe; they gained the confidence that they could do the same for their own students.

First, one of the teachers led a brainstorming session about their assumptions and questions about air and wrote their responses on the board:

Cool air is heavier	How do you weigh air?
Warm air rises	How do you warm air? Cool it? How much?
Gas laws	Does it matter if you measure first, then heat or cool it?
Athletes at high altitudes need more red blood cells	Should we measure volume and/or mass?
	What is relationship between volume and density?
	How to measure air?
	Should liquid or vapor be used?
	What are the constants?
	What makes something hot?
	How is energy expressed as heat?

They divided into groups and each set out to develop an inquiry lesson that would engage their students' interest while also responding to the question, *Which is heavier, cold air or ward air?*

SMALL GROUPS

Group 1

This group used balloons to explore the question. Using two balloons, they sought a way to look at changes in volume as temperature changes. They blew up two balloons and immersed each in water (at room temperature) to measure displacement and ensure that the two balloons had roughly the same volume. They then placed one balloon in a refrigerator to cool; the other remained at room temperature. After the refrigerated balloon had chilled, they attempted to immerse the balloons again, this time in warm water with the idea that they would measure changes in the amount of water displaced. However, the chilled balloon broke before it was even immersed. They hypothesized that either the water was hot enough to expand the air and pop the balloon or something in the substance of the balloon itself caused it to burst.

As they presented their experiment to the larger group, questions arose about the fact that they were examining buoyancy and density as opposed to mass. A discussion followed about what each of those terms meant. What was becoming clearer and clearer to the teachers was that the recipe approach represented a very narrow way of looking at larger issues—that it would, in fact, cut off rather than encourage curiosity and intellectual and creative inquiry.

Group 2

This group sought to replicate the textbook recipe by using the same materials as prescribed. They set up a free scale with two bags attached on either end of a yardstick and used a flame to heat the air in one of the open bags.

The bag that was heated barely rose, so they increased the amount of time for heating. Still, there was very little difference. However, once they closed the top of the bag and held the flame underneath, there was a considerable tilt to their scale. It seemed clear that the heated air had caused the bag to rise and that, therefore, hot air was lighter than cool air, until they removed the flame and saw the scale return to an earlier position with just a slight tilt in the direction of the heated bag. One of the teachers commented that perhaps it was the flame itself that was responsible for causing the bag to rise. Further questions arose about whether the bags should be open, like hot air balloons, or closed. They then decided to do the experiment again with two closed bags. The results were again unclear.

The teachers were not sure what they had learned from this experiment. They realized they would have to run it several times, precisely measure changes in the scale's movement, and perhaps use bags made out of other materials. The experiment was supposed to be proof that hot air is lighter, but it did not take into account the variables they had discovered in trying to execute it.

Group 3

This group pondered the use of baking soda and vinegar to generate a gas, but as they began to discuss the problems they would encounter, they realized that air was already present in test tubes. This greatly simplified their design. They weighed two tubes and capped one; both were then placed in the refrigerator. Both were later removed and weighed again. Their assumption was that the open tube now had warmer air moving in and out and so would now weigh more. But when they weighed the two tubes, there was a difference of only 0.1 gram. The realized they would have to redo their experiment, perhaps using a more sensitive scale to measure the difference in weight. If the mass was changing because of the incoming air particles and kinetic energy, perhaps they needed to change the procedure for capping one of the tubes.

PEDAGOGICAL CONCERNS At this point, after hearing all the presentations, one of the teachers involved the whole group in a larger discussion about the experiments and what they were trying to prove. They wondered if perhaps the question needed to be clearer; they felt they first needed to show that air mass has properties before they could show changes in its weight with changes in temperature. They were, in essence, trying to find a way to prove what they already knew, and that presented difficulties for them. Why test something we already know? Why ask students to test something we already know? And if we do ask students to create knowledge about something that we think we already know, isn't it more difficult not to intervene?

They recognized the difficulty of bringing a molecular problem to a visual level and questioned whether they could come up with adequate experiments. But during their debate about density, volume and mass, they reached a critical conclusion—that the recipe experiment cited in the text did not test what it was supposed to test! They realized the experiments they were planning measured density but not mass.

They questioned what their terms meant: What is lightness vs. heaviness? What does mass mean, if we're not talking about buoyancy or density?Maybe, they conjectured, that was the whole point of the lesson, to raise questions about what might seem already obvious to us. As one teacher commented, this is "making me think really hard . . . we have to make sure we're using the words in the right way. What does heavy mean?" What had originally seemed quite simple turned into a complex problem.

The teachers were concerned that their students would be too frustrated not only by an experiment like this, which didn't seem to prove anything, but by the whole questioning process that emerges when trying to figure out why it didn't prove anything. But the group leader pointed out that kids understand the concepts even if they don't have the scientific terminology to define what they know. For example, they understand density, even if they can't name it, and they know a heated balloon gets bigger.

Kids often have the information, but teachers need to give them the opportunities to draw on it. In a genetics class, for example, students don't need to discuss Mendel's experiments before solving a genetics problem. In an animal behavior class, to cite another example, students can figure out ways to measure an animal's intelligence by using the scientific method before they know the specialized language used in the field.

One teacher mentioned that he takes his students to Central Park as part of a science project and phrases his question simply: Is the pond experiencing problems? Students are capable of doing research, collecting samples, and asking questions about the pond, even if they don't have a fully developed scientific language with which to frame their discussion. Even so, teachers worried if students knew enough to ask good questions and critique each other's work. Once again, the focus of the group came back to how do we get students to be more analytical.

THE INQUIRY SUMMARY

Inquiry is highly structured and planned out, even if the surface appearance may give a different impression. At this point in the process, once the experiments are completed and students have had time to question, discuss, and debate, what does a teacher need to do to help them gain clarity about what they have learned?

Part of the teacher's role, as mentioned earlier, is to walk around the room taking notes while students are in groups and during discussion. The teacher then shares these notes with the students, summarizing the outcomes of what has occurred and highlighting the areas that still need to be investigated. When students read this inquiry summary and see, in writing, the results of their groups' discussion and work, they learn to value their contributions and focus on what needs to be done next.

The group leader modeled the process for the teachers by beginning each day with an inquiry summary of the previous day's outcomes and a focus for the day's activities. Below is an example:

> We were trying to figure out how to respond to the question *Which is heavier, cold air or warm air?* We tried setting up experiments, but we found out that we had to change our plan. We weren't measuring mass but volume. How would we have to change our question? Is a weight change measured by heaviness or density? What kind of experiment should we set up next?

The group leader discussed the use of recipe-type approaches to physics problems that are readily available in all physics textbooks. Using these recipes is a viable way of planning, but be forewarned that something always shows up in these experiments that is unexpected. This can provide a natural way to begin inquiry: If the book tells us one thing, why have we wound up with something else?

For example, in the group leader's physics classes, the students never get 9.8 as their measurement for gravity (they get anywhere from 5 to 20). This presents students with questions to explore: Why don't they reach the accepted number for gravity? What happens when groups get opposite results to an experiment?

That's when the thinking begins. In the physics case, the group leader presented the students with three different texts to show how each arrives at a different conclusion. In the inquiry summary, a number of questions would be posed for the students to help them focus their next activity:

> How do we redefine our experiment?
> How do we look up what we need to know?
> How do we redo the experiment?
> Do we need a new question?

All this involves extensive planning not only for the students but for the teacher, as well.

Other Pedagogical Concerns

THE LAB REPORT

The group got back to basics when discussing lab reports. They questioned its purpose and its format. In particular, the group focused on the discussion section of the lab report. Is it a summary of what you've done? A reflection of what you've learned? An assertion of your hypothesis? Does contradictory information get included, regardless of its relevancy to the original hypothesis? Is a hypothesis a question? What is the difference between the discussion section and the conclusion?

They debated whether the hypothesis is an assertion you try to make afterward or the result of *other* work you have done—playing with possibilities, observing, learning information—which is then tested. One teacher cautioned that it is critical to begin with a clearly stated hypothesis to know what it is you are testing; if you develop it too late, it is no longer a hypothesis. The question is what you are testing and the hypothesis is what you think will happen though, as another teacher reflected on the groups' experiments together, you don't always know what it is you are trying to do.

The teachers did agree, however, that scientists have been remarkably consistent in their approach to the lab report. Its basic purpose is to present an experiment that can be replicated. Hypotheses must be stated, procedures must be detailed.

They discussed ways to motivate students to keep good notes during their lab work. Some of the teachers admitted that during the experiment with the floating penny, knowing that the group leader already knew the "right" answer made them less careful about recording their data. In contrast, for their horticulture experiment, since there was no right answer stored somewhere, they were more scrupulous about maintaining data that could be helpful later on.

READING IN THE SCIENCES

Textbooks The teachers said they would like their students to complete more readings in the sciences but weren't sure if textbooks would be useful in an inquiry classroom. The group leader pointed out the benefit of using many textbooks, not one. In this way, students would see that different texts present information in different ways, and one text may have an explanation that doesn't conform to another text's version. This provides a potential question and hypothesis for students to explore and experiment with.

Other texts In addition to the traditional textbooks, science teachers can provide a wide range of reading materials for their students, including articles from the weekly science section of *The New York Times* to magazines like *Consumer Reports* and *Newsweek* to longer books and novels (such as *When Elephants Cry* by S. McCarthy and J. Moussaieff, *Never Cry Wolf* by Farley Mowat, *Call of the Wild* by Jack London, and James Herriot's *Dog and Cat Stories*).

FOLLOW UP

Though the calendar and sunlight said July, the teachers began to think September and thought about what they themselves might plan for their fall semester classes. The process was a lengthy one and yielded sketches of a few possibilities:

Mapping

One teacher would be teaching 9th grade earth science in the fall. His interests ranged from geology to meteorology and oceanography. For this exercise, to come up with an inquiry lesson that might be helpful for his class, he focused on mapping, particularly contour mapping. Out of this, he framed the question: *How do we show heights on a flat piece of paper?* Some ideas that he and others in the group generated are below:

- Set up columns of books in the classroom, each at one of five different heights. Ask the students to then draw a map of the room and find a way to make clear the contours of the book-columns. They would have to measure distances between the columns as well as the degree of the slopes on both sides.
- Build a Lego sculpture with varying heights and then draw it for someone else on a flat surface. The color of the Lego pieces would change as the height of each entity changed.

Microbiology

Taking the group leader's advice to "work backwards," one teacher's idea was to have students conduct an experiment based on a previous experiment in microbiology. For the first experiment, then, she proposed a gallery of "stuff" arranged in stations that would greet students when they entered the room:

Petri dishes with bugs	liquid cultures	Supplies: wax
selections of fresh food	baker's yeast	plastic wrap
selections of rotten food	slides of bacteria	gloves

Students would be asked to group the items in a variety of different ways. Then they would grow bacteria and count them. Out of that would develop questions about how the bacteria reproduce and why.

This teacher fashioned her approach according to what she had learned through the workshop. When she had been looking through textbooks for examples of recipes, she had found one that focused on sterilizing carrots and then infecting them with a particular microbe, which could also be stained and looked at under the microscope. But with an inquiry approach to this experiment, she noted that "what's important seems to shift when you turn things around." For example, with this experiment, "when it's turned around to ask What makes food go bad? it doesn't matter so much which microbe it is or what stain you need to see it. Instead, we would explore what microorganisms are in our actual environments, and find out together some ways to perceive them."

Chemistry

Two teachers went to a sourcebook to gather and try out ideas. They consulted *Inquiry and Problem-Solving in the Physical Sciences: A Sourcebook* (V. Lunetta and S. Novick, Kendall/Hunt Publishing Co., Dubuque, IA). Their interest is in chemistry, and they played with the idea of beginning with a study of the phases of matter by focusing on the question: Which freezes faster, hot water or cold water? From there, students would develop their hypotheses and questions, which might include:

What should the initial temperature of the freezer be?
What temperature should the liquid be?
What size should the container be? How many should be used?
Should the freezer be empty?
How pure is the water?
What should be the gap in temperature between the hot and cold water?
How do you know something is frozen all the way through?

A Lesson for All Seasons

All the participating teachers came away from the workshop with the confidence that they could use an inquiry approach in their classrooms. They themselves had experienced first-hand the value of active learning, the freedom to experiment with ideas and materials, the important role that discussion and debate play in understanding and clarifying what has been learned, and the pleasure that being engaged with original research can provide.

As one teacher wrote in her reflection on the workshop, "my brain was always *on*."

A P P E N D I X

CHAPTER 3   From Recipe to Inquiry: Chemistry Experiment

"Floating Pennies" experiment from *Chemical Activities: Teacher Edition* by Christie L. Borford and Lee R. Summerlin (American Chemical Society: Washington D.C.) 1988.

CHAPTER 4   Research and Research Design

"Effects of Diets High in Sucrose or Aspartame on the Behavior and Cognitive Performance of Children" by M. Wolraich, M.D., S. Lindgren, Ph.D., P. Stumbo, Ph.D., L Stegink, Ph.D., Mark Appelbaum, Ph. D., and M. Kiritsy, M.Sc., R.D. *New England Journal of Medicene*, 330(5), 301-7, 1994.

CHAPTER 5   From Recipe to Inquiry: Physics Experiment

Information on the UNESCO publication: *700 Science Experiments for Everyone.* (1958) New York: Doubleday.

RESOURCES
Suggested by members of the summer workshop

Below is a list of resources—books, web sites, professional organizations—suggested by the teachers who participated in the summer workshop.

Books:

Bloomfield, L. A. (1997) *How Things Work: The Physics of Everyday Life.* New York: John Wiley & Sons, Inc.

Borgford, C. and L. R. Summerlin. (1988). *Chemical Activities (Teacher Edition).* Washington, DC: American Chemical Society.

Cassidy, J. (1991) *Explorabook: A Kids Science Museum in a Book.* Palo Alto, CA: Klutz Press.

Chang, R. (1997) *Chemistry* McGraw-Hill.

Council for Environmental Education. (1998) *Project WET.* Montana State University. Bozeman

Dalmatz, M. S., H. K. Wong. (1971). *Physical Science Ideas and Investigations in Science (Teachers Manual).* Englewood Cliffs, NJ: Prentice-Hall, Inc.

Djerassi, C., and R. Hoffman. (2001). *Oxygen: A Play in 2 Acts.* New York: Wiley-VCH.

Evironmental Science, Addison Wesley, Publisher.

Faber, A., E. Mazlish, L. Nyberg, and R.A. Templeton. *How to Talk so Kids Can Learn: At Home and in School.* Simon and Schuster Trade

Haskel, S. and D. Sygoda. (1973) *Biology Investigations.* New York: Amsco School Publications.

Hewitt, P. (1997) *Conceptual Physics.* Upper Saddle River, NJ: Pentice Hall

Hogan, K. (1994) *Eco-Inquiry.* Dubuque, IA: Kendal/Hunt Publishing Co. (Excellent source of units, with inquiry-based assessments, rubrics and experiments.

Kaplan, E. H. (1983) *Problem Solving in Biology—Incorporating Experiences in Life Science 3rd. ed.* New York: Macmillan Publishing Co., Inc.

Krause, L.M. (1994) *Fear of Physics*. Basic Books.

Lunetta, V. N. and S. Novick. (1982). *Inquiry and Problem-Solving in the Physical Sciences,* Dubuque, IA: Kendall/Hunt Publishing Co.

McGee. H. (1997) *On Food and Cooking: The Science and Lore of the Kitchen.* Simon and Schuster Trade.

Petrides, G.A. (1972) *Peterson Field Guids—Trees and Shrubs.* New York: Houghton Mifflin Co.

National Research Council Staff. (1995) *National Science Education Standards: Observe, Interact, Change, Learn.* Washington, DC: National Academy of Sciences.

Phillips. (1997) *Chemistry: Concepts and Application.* McGraw Hill.

Spanning, N. E. (1989) *Earth Science Laboratory Investigations.* Lexington, MA: D.C. Heath and Compay.

Summerlin, L.R. and J. L.Ealy. (1988) *Chemical Demonstrations: A Sourcebook for Teachers Volume 1, 2nd Ed.* Washington, DC: Amercian Chemical Society.

Summerlin, L.R. , C.L. Borgford and J. B.Ealy. (1988) *Chemical Demonstrations: A Sourcebook for Teachers Volume 2, 2nd Ed.* Washington, DC: Amercian Chemical Society.

UNESCO, ed. *700 Science Experiments for Everyone.* (1958) New York: Doubleday.

Walker, P. and E. Wood. (1994). *Hands-On General Science Activities with Real Life Applications.* West Nyack, NY: The Center for Applied Research in Education.

Other Resources:

Teacher Association Websites:

Amercian Association of Physics Teachers http://www.aapt.org/

American Chemical Society http://www.acs.org/

National Earth Science Teachers Association http://soe.csusb.edu/nesta/

National Association of Biology Teachers http://www.nabt.org/

National Science Teachers Association http://www.nsta.org/

Other Websites:

http://www.TroutintheClassroom.com

The website for an excellent program called Trout in the Classroom. Raising trout in the classroom can be an excellent resource for inquiry-based exploration.

http://www.nypl.org—The New York City Public Library

http://www3.infotrieve.com/medline/infotrieve/—A Free Medline Search Engine

http://www4.nationalacademies.org/nas/nashome.nsf—National Academy of Sciences

http://www.itv.scetv.org/—Instructional Television, State Department of Education
They have a resource books and program schedules.

Places to Go, Things to Do

American Museum of Natural History
http://www.amnh.org/
(There is also a library there)

Central Park Conservancy
http://www.centralparknyc.org/
(212) 360-2722
(212) 360-2764

Liberty Science Center
http://www.lsc.org/
Liberty State Park
Jersey City, NJ 07305
201-200-1000

Medical Library Center of New York
http://www.mlcny.lib.ny.us/
5 East 102 Street, 7th Floor
New York, NY 10029
(212) 427-1630

New York Hall of Science
http://www.nyhallsci.org/
47-01 111th Street, Flushing Meadows
Corona Park, New York 11368
718.699.0005

Brooklyn Botanic Garden
http://www.bbg.org/
1000 Washington Avenue
Brooklyn, NY 11225
(718) 623-7200

New York Botanic Garden
http://www.nybg.org/
The New York Botanical Garden
200th St. and Kazimiroff Blvd.
Bronx, New York 10458
(718) 817-8700
Classes and composting available to
teachers during the summer

Lower East Side Ecology Center
(212) 477-4022
(212) 420-0621
Purveyors of compost and worms

Also:
**Green Apple Tour of NYC's East
Village & Lower East Side**
http://www.greenmap.com/grmaps/nycev.html

AN INQUIRY COURSE:
ANIMAL BEHAVIOR

BARRY J. FOX • Illustrations by David Fox

"Where do we begin? What exactly is animal behavior? The answer cannot be straight-forward and simple. Roughly speaking, behavior is the movements animals make. This involves more than running, swimming, crawling or other types of locomotion. It also includes the movements animals make when feeding, when mating, or even when breathing. Even slight movements of parts of the body, such as pricking the ears or making a sound, are also parts of behavior. And of course behavior can also consist of standing still and looking intently or perhaps just thinking – doing something internal-ly that may influence subsequent behavior.

"The behavior of most animals is not completely known. But enough is alread known to set us wondering about what it all means, to ask questions about behavior: and this nat-ural progression from description to inquiry leads us deeper and deeper into the subject."

NIKO TINBERGEN (world famous animal behaviorist)

Introduction

When I first developed my Animal Behavior course, I isolated some of the long-range goals for the course, including the major goal of getting the kids to understand how scientists go about solving problems. I wanted the students to internalize the scientific method. The crucial question then became how to achieve this goal. How could I get kids to think scientifically, to work through research designs? How could I make this course different from a traditional science class? How could I make it an inquiry class?

This course evolved "backwards," since I always know where I want the students to end up. For a final project, I wanted them to work in small groups to study one of the kinds of animals I had in the classroom. They would have to define a specific problem, formulate appropriate hypotheses, collect, record, and interpret data, and arrive at conclusions consistent with their findings.

I will discuss here my experiences with one particular class in order to illustrate more clearly students' development from the beginning of a course to the end. Of course, every class is different, but what I discuss here is basically representative of the kinds of experiences that unfold across these classes.

In this class, the six groups in the class made varying degrees of progress on the animal behavior project. Each group had developed a research design without direct teacher intervention, and according to a visiting teacher of animal behavior, each of the projects was "relevant, clearly defined, and had appropriate controls." The important point to make here is that it was the students themselves (working in small groups) that had designed and carried out the animal projects. When asked on an end term evaluation if they could have done this in the beginning of the semester, they invariably responded that they would not have been able to conduct an experiment themselves.

Such results do not come easily. The course must be constructed so that students quickly come to feel comfortable with experimentation. They must consider themselves scientists. The course could be divided into the following three phases, each lasting about three weeks:

Establishing an atmosphere for inquiry
Planning and executing the class project
Planning and executing projects in small groups

The inquiry lesson differs from the developmental lesson in some very fundamental ways, which makes it difficult to talk about in terms of self-contained daily lessons. Each inquiry lesson is not necessarily completed in a 45-minute time span, and ideas are often left up in the air at the end of class time. It becomes the teacher's job to process what has happened and return it to the students the next day so that they can then move forward with the investigation. Rather than describing an inquiry course on a day-by-day lesson basis, it is probably more useful to describe the class's activities, the reasons behind those particular activities, and the students' responses to the different assignments.

BARRY J. FOX

1

Establishing an Atmosphere

The first thing that I want to do is to see how well the students can formulate questions. Since animal behavior begins with observation, I combined these two skills—observation and questioning—into the following activity. I set up tanks housing different animals: hooded rats, gerbils, ants (an ant farm), earthworms, hamsters, frogs, snakes, lizards (anoles) and fish. In this class, next to each "station," I hung blank poster board. I gave the class the following directions:

> Divide yourselves into groups of no more than three, with one group at each "station." Observe the behavior of the animals for ten minutes. On the poster next to the tank, write any questions you have about the animals' behavior. Write your name next to your question. After ten minutes, each group will then proceed to the next tank to the right. Repeat these instructions for that tank and then continue around the room in this way.

Some students were unable to think of questions about an animal, although they were busy observing. To push them to write, I told them to describe what they saw the animal doing, and then, focusing on one particular aspect of the animal's behavior, figure out what about that behavior they would like to know more about.

The class was actively involved in this exercise. They were all walking around the room, observing animals, and writing down questions. The students appeared to enjoy the activity, as well. Even after class was over, the kids were still looking around, calling each other's attention to particular animals. There was a genuine excitement. However, no one actually observed a particular tank of animals for five minutes, let alone for ten minutes. After just one or two minutes of observing (or even a shorter time, for some), the students wrote their questions and moved on to any other tank that interested them. Still, the class of 24 students managed to generate over 90 different questions covering all of the animals in the room. (See the Notes section for a complete list of all the questions generated.)

The majority of the questions were not very thoughtful or insightful. Most seemed to be based upon random curiosity about an animal, rather than actual observation of that animal. For example, 21 different gerbil questions were generated, including the following:

- How old are the gerbils?
- How do all the babies fit inside the little gerbil?
- How do you tell the male from the female?
- How many babies do they have at one time?
- How does the female carry her babies?
- What's the difference between a hamster and a gerbil?
- What's the difference between a gerbil and a mouse?

The hooded rats generated the following questions:

- Why do they call them hooded rats?
- Do they bite?
- Will they get any bigger?
- Do hooded rats eat any food?

I wanted my students to begin to analyze the quality of their questions. In class the next day, I distributed a compiled list of their questions. I divided the class into small groups and, using only the gerbil questions, asked each group to choose the best and the worst questions and to explain the reasons for their choices. I did not give them any criteria upon which to base their decisions of "best" and "worst."

The students had difficulty with this task. After a short time, I brought them together for a discussion of the problems they were having. I asked them to define the differences among the following questions: How long does it take for a baby gerbil to open its eyes? How does the mother gerbil know which is her baby? and What happens to a gerbil when it is out of its cage? As a result of the discussion, the class decided that there were two types of questions: those for which answers can be found in a book and those for which answers needed "experimentation" (their word, and I did not push the word "research" at this time). I asked them to return to the list of 92 questions to determine which other ones would require "experimentation." The students again worked in small groups to list the various types of questions. Each group then decided upon their best two questions and added them to a master list of questions that the class compiled on the board. The master list included the following questions:

- What kind of food does the gerbil eat?
- Does the cold have an effect on gerbils?
- How does the mother know which is her baby?
- What happens to a gerbil when it is out of his cage?
- What colors can gerbils see?
- Why does a chameleon change colors?
- Do lizards use their tails for anything special?
- How long does it take for the chameleon's color to change?
- Can a lizard survive in all types of weather?
- Why do the fish seem to follow one another?
- Do hamsters get along with gerbils?
- Why is the hamster so mean?
- How can the ants pick up the grains of sand?
- Why do ants build tunnels?
- Can ants form communities?

Once we had this master list I encouraged students to continue to debate the quality of some of them. There were some questions that could perhaps be answered by a book, but they still might require research. One such example was, "What colors can a gerbil see?" As one student pointed out, "You might be able to locate this answer in a book, but how does the book know?"

This seemed to me a good time to see how much the class knew about how an experiment might be performed, since the students were beginning to think about that spontaneously. I asked them how they would set up an experiment to answer the question about color perception in gerbils. As it turned out, they did-n't have a clue as to how to structure a valid experiment that would address the problem. Had this not been an inquiry class, I probably would have given them a step-by-step procedure to set up an experiment. Instead, I gave them no answers and decided to pursue the analysis of their questions. I selected the following two questions from their master list:

Why does a chameleon (anole) change color?
How long does it take for the chameleon's color to change?

I began by asking what the class thought of these two research questions. After a brief discussion, it was agreed that the first question was "better" because they would have to experiment in order to arrive at an answer. To answer the second question, all they would have to do is "just sit there and watch." Although they were unable to verbalize it in a sophisticated way, the students were establishing criteria for what makes a good question. They had determined that open-ended questions were better research questions than ones for which there was only one right answer, or about which there was nothing to dispute.

HYPOTHESIZING

I asked the class to brainstorm for possible answers to the "better" question. They arrived at the following five possibilities:

A Chameleon Might Change Color When:

1. The color of its surroundings (environment) changes, so it needs to camouflage itself.
2. The temperature of its environment changes.
3. It is feeding.
4. Its mood changes (when it is fighting, or angry, or when it is calm).
5. A male is attracting a female.

At this point, I explained that the process of guessing at answers was known as "hypothesizing," while a guess itself was called a "hypothesis." These words were definitely new to most students, but the class instantly adopted the terms. They liked using these new words whenever there was a class discussion. The terms held real meaning for them now. The students were making hypotheses, as opposed to being told that hypothesizing is something that scientists do. An atmosphere of serious scientific inquiry had been established, and it was beginning to affect the kids.

Next, I wanted the class to play with one of their hypotheses. I intentionally use the word "play," and I don't want the reader to misunderstand, particularly in light of the serious atmosphere that had just been established in the classroom. Students are rarely given the opportunity to play with ideas because educators tend to be in a great hurry for kids to learn some piece of information or to get an answer. Yet, many scientific discoveries were made as a direct result of intellectual play. In that spirit, I asked the class to think about the hypothesis that temperature affected the chameleon's color change. How could we test this hypothesis? Working in small groups, the students tried to develop an experimental design, or a way of finding out whether temperature could be a factor in the color changes they had observed. The groups struggled with this for a few minutes before we came together to exchange ideas:

MIKE: We should start with one tank and put in 6 chameleons and raise the temperature to 90 degrees.

THOMAS: Maybe they're affected by cold instead of heat, so we should fill in another tank and lower the temperature.

LYNN: How do you lower the temperature?

ISMAEL: We need something to keep the temperature from changing.

MIKE: Okay. We'll use a light bulb to raise the temperature and shut it off to lower the temperature.

CHRIS: But then how do you know that the chameleon is changing color because of the temperature? Maybe it's the light that makes him change color.

Although they weren't using the technical language, the kids were certainly beginning to consider how variables affect results. They were even hinting at the use of a control by the end of the class discussion. The following design-oriented questions arose from class debate:

1. How many chameleons would we need?
2. How many tanks would we need?
3. How many chameleons would we put in each tank?
4. What should be the temperature in each tank?
5. What should we put in each tank (wood, pebble, plants, nothing)?
6. Should the chameleons be fed? If so, what and how much?
7. Should we put chameleons of opposite sexes together?
8. How long should we do this experiment? How will we know when to stop?

The class argued each of these points. Sometimes, the evidence they used in support of arguments was not clearly thought through or was otherwise weak. However, the following significant comments were made:

1. We should put the same number of chameleons in each tank.
2. One of the tanks should be at room temperature.
3. We should have something that keeps the different temperatures in the tanks steady. (They did not use the word "thermostat," but that was obviously what they meant.)
4. We should put the same things in each tank. They should also be of the same color.

INQUIRY SUMMARY

I reproduced all of the questions and comments that resulted from this discussion and distributed them to the class the following day. This was the first time that I had given the class any written feedback from a discussion. I think it is very important at this point to explain why I think this is a valuable classroom strategy. First of all, classes are generally surprised to receive the notes. They were unaware that I had been taking notes during the class discussion—they said they thought I had been doing homework. The students liked seeing the name of the person who had asked each question. This tactic improved the follow-up discussions because it enabled kids to talk more to each other and less often to me. My classes usually seem surprised about the contents of the notes—surprised that they have actually stated these ideas and that those ideas are important and useful.

This strategy of teacher note-taking can be considered an "inquiry summary," a very different exercise from the traditional developmental lesson's medial summary. Teacher notes can be used to help kids see inquiry as a process. Through notes, it becomes apparent that ideas were presented, that disagreements occurred, and that arguments were both defended and criticized. In a science class, attention can be focused on kids' different approaches to designing experiments and testing hypotheses.

In the discussion that followed the recorded class discussion, I emphasized that the class had been tackling a fundamental problem of scientific research: how to eliminate extraneous variables when testing a given hypothesis, including the establishment of valid controls. We connected the meanings of "variables" and "controls" with the class's questions and comments from the previous day. I reminded them that the issue of how to control the variables in an experiment came out of their discussion of how best to solve the chameleon problem. I had never suggested that the class set up a control tank. My role had been to facilitate the discussion, or, as one student put it, "to make us think about what we were doing."

Eventually, I want my classes to set up animal behavior experiments using the animals in our classroom. In the beginning of the term, I therefore ask the kids to submit (on almost a daily basis) short proposals describing possible research projects. I ask each of them to think of a question about a particular animal, figure out an experiment that would help to answer that question, and finally to describe any problems that might arise during that experiment. In this class, this assignment met with very little success. I had anticipated this difficulty, especially because the students weren't quite sure what I was asking of them. The following project proposals illustrate some of the difficulties the students encountered:

Student A

QUESTION: How big or long does the snake grow?

PROJECT: I can answer this question by reading or looking in a book about snakes.

Student B

QUESTION: When can baby gerbils start to reproduce?

HYPOTHESIS: I guess they can start reproducing when they are 7 months old.

PROJECT: I take a 7-month female gerbil and I take a male gerbil and see what happens. I would put both gerbils in a fish tank with food and water for at least one week and observe. The problem that I might have with this observation is that the female gerbil might not get pregnant.

Student C

QUESTION: Could gerbils be trained? What colors do they see?

PROJECT: I would buy a gerbil and get him used to me, then try to train him. Also, I would put different colors in front of him to see which one he goes up to. I might have problems trying to train him because I don't think that they are easy to train.

A QUESTIONING PATTERN

Many students were unable to independently formulate valid experimental designs. In order to focus their thinking as well as to help them see the range of possible projects, I had the class perform the following exercise. I chose one of their 92 listed questions—"Do hooded rats eat any food?"—and asked them to think of as many related questions as possible. The discussion that followed was extremely important and demonstrates how the inquiry process works.

After a short period of silence, the kids offered a quick list of three or four questions. Then there was another period of silence, a bit longer than the first, followed by a few more questions.

Doing the same exercise during an inquiry science workshop for teachers interested in how inquiry would work within a standard curriculum, such as that prescribed by the New York State Board of Regents, I found that the question development process occurred similarly. The topic was the breathing mechanisms in the grasshopper and they were asked to generate questions about grasshopper behavior after they had watched a grasshopper breathe for several minutes. I reproduce their questions here to demonstrate the process.

The questions were generated in the following order:

1. Where does the air go in?
2. Do they breathe air?

(Period of silence)

3. Does the air go in the blood?
4. Do they have blood?
5. Where does the air come out?
6. What is air for?
7. What part of air do they breathe?
8. What is air?

(Period of silence)

9. How much do they breathe?
10. Does breathing increase during strenuous exercise?

The general pattern of questioning in this example is typical of students in my Animal Behavior course. For example, the first questions posed by my students tend to have one-word answers, just as the teachers' questions 2 and 3 can be answered by either "Yes" or "No." Most of the remaining questions posed by the students require descriptive (as opposed to analytical) answers. A rough sequence to the questions is generally discernable, in that earlier questions clearly prompt those that follow. For example, question 3 was generated only after 2 was asked, and 4 was clearly triggered by question 3.

As the question listing exercise proceeds, there is often a shift in the quality of the questions. Numbers 7, 9, and 10 lend themselves to a hypothesis-testing approach, as opposed to the earlier questions, which are easily answered by an encyclopedia. Individual participants even posed better and better questions as the exercise proceeded. The same teacher who asked question 1 asked the tenth question.

The most thoughtful questions, numbers 9 and 10 above, were stated only after the teachers were allowed to pause to quietly think. The silent periods gave the teachers the time necessary to think of better questions—questions requiring research.

I did not interrupt the group during the brainstorming process. The order of the questions shows that the teachers were listening to one another and incorporating new information and ideas into their new questions. After a third silent period, I asked them how question 10 could have been better phrased. They changed it to, "How does strenuous exercise affect the breathing rate?" This led to a discussion that raised the following points:

1. How do you define "breathing" in a grasshopper? What is one breath?
2. How do you define "strenuous exercise" for a grasshopper? Strenuous compared to what? What's the control?
3. How would you measure breathing rates? How many measurements would you take before finding the average?

Through a similar questioning exercise in my Animal Behavior class, the question, "Do hooded rats eat any food?" evolved into an experimental design that addressed the question, "What is the effect of different drinks on the behavior of the hooded rat?"

During the first couple of weeks of that class, I strove to improve my students' questioning skills. The next set of activities is intended to further develop the class's research abilities.

2

Class Project

EARTHWORMS

Next, I had the whole class work in small, independent groups to study earthworms. Rather than have each group study a different animal and then report their findings to the whole group, I elected to have all groups study the same animal in order to emphasize the concept that there are many different approaches to the same problem. Earthworms seemed appropriate because students are familiar with them, and because the worms would be inexpensive, easy to maintain, and very active. I did not predetermine how long the class would work with the worms, nor could I have predicted how the exercise would evolve. As it turned out, the earthworm experience became a cornerstone for subsequent classes.

On the first earthworm day, I gave each group the following instructions, along with a tray containing three or four live earthworms:

Find out as much about the behavior of these worms as possible. You may have anything you need from the lab as long as you explain how you plan to use it.

All of your observations must be recorded. You must also list any questions you have about the earthworms' behavior.

It was interesting to watch the different groups' reactions to the trays of worms. Some of the groups immediately began to record observations. These groups did not hesitate to handle the worms. Other groups were repulsed by the worms, and one group threatened to leave the classroom. After looking at the worms for a few minutes, however, someone in that group decided to poke the worms with a probe in order to see their response. Luckily, the worms were very active and responsive, so the other members of the group gradually overcame their negative feelings and became increasingly curious. Some students still refused to touch the worms, though. These students usually became recording secretaries for their groups. After about fifteen minutes, all students were actively involved in the exercise, and everyone seemed to be having a good time for the rest of the hour.

I noticed at least one major change in the class compared with their behavior the previous week: they spent more time observing and writing than they had spent on the first day's exercise. When they were moving from tank to tank, observing and writing questions during the opening activity, they hadn't spent more than five minutes per tank. This time, however, many of them were busily observing for the entire hour.

Although they had been asked to list questions as well as record observations, the students had for the most part just recorded observations. With the exception of one group that requested a beaker of water, the groups did not request additional equipment from the lab. I had not told them what equipment was available to them because I didn't want to influence their methods. I had hoped that each group would consider what other items or tools might by useful for their study.

The class reassembled, and we collectively developed a list of over 30 different observations of the earthworms' behavior. The following day, I distributed their list of observations to the class:

1. Stretches out
2. Moves faster in the water
3. Not used to its new environment
4. It feels its way around
5. Doesn't like water
6. It is like it has two heads
7. Muscles contract so it can move
8. From the time it was placed in the tray until now, it has become a lighter color

9. Moves rapidly—the head first and squirms the rest of the body along
10. Moves in a circle
11. When it is touched, it forms a ball
12. It moves straight
13. When cut in half, both sides still move
14. They feel pain (This observation came from the group that cut the worm in half.)
15. All of a sudden, it has gotten very long
16. Looks like the worm finds the pan a strange place
17. When touched, it curls up
18. The body expands and draws up
19. He is sensitive
20. He wants to get away from us
21. He moves the front half of the body, then brings in the back
22. Doesn't want to come out of the water
23. When we took him out of the water, he went back in the water
24. Moves both ends before it moves
25. Turns like a cobra
26. Has three shades of color
27. Has white bumps
28. It is darker in the front
29. Has red blood
30. Has a flat end and a fat end
31. Skin looks slimy and wet

Their observations could be roughly divided into three categories: external observations of form, texture, and color; observations of locomotive behavior; and observations of worms' responses to stimuli. I never mentioned these categories to the class. Instead, I used the categories to sort out the types of observations my students were making.

I was very pleased to see that only 6 of the 31 observations fell into the first category, describing morphology rather than behavior. Many of the observations centered instead around the worms' movements, and one group went so far as to time those movements.

By piecing together all of the various motor observations, the class arrived at an interesting hypothesis regarding the adaptive value of earthworm locomotion. The students agreed that there must be two sets of muscles in the worm which enable it to move the way it does. After some discussion, the class decided that having two sets of muscles might enable the worm to move more easily in its natural environment, underground.

ANTHROPOMORPHISM

The class felt that they had done a very thorough job, but I wanted them to analyze their observations more critically. I directed them to the following "observations" (inferences, actually) that they had recorded:

The worm doesn't like water.
He wants to get away from us.

I asked the class what questions they would want to ask the person(s) who had made these observations. The following exchange resulted:

MARILYN: How do you know he doesn't like water?

IVAN: He moved away from it.

ME: That's the observation: the worm moves away from water. It's not that he doesn't like water.

After further probing, the question of "proof"—or, "how do you know"—finally arose. The students who had made these inferential "observations" had to explain what they had actually observed that led them to make those inferences. Consequently, remarks such as, "The worm doesn't like water" became "The worm moved to the opposite end of the tray from the water." Likewise, "He wants to get away from us" became "He moved to the opposite end of the tray from our hands."

At this time, I chose to introduce the technical term "anthropomorphism" (ascribing human qualities to nonhuman life) because it would now mean something to the students. It wouldn't just be an abstract term to memorize; instead, it would describe simply and precisely what they had discovered on their own. When I asked the class to find other examples of anthropomorphism, they pinpointed observations number 3 and 22. As a result, I became aware of the extent to which the kids were questioning each other, without my involvement.

I separated the class into small groups and asked them to find more examples of anthropomorphism. I also instructed them to compile a list of the observations that required further explanation. They made the following list of observations for which they required more proof:

> It looks like the worm finds the pan a strange place.
> He is sensitive.
> They feel pain.

The period was over and, as I considered how to proceed the following day, I realized that several important issues had arisen. The students had begun to ask how accurate a behavioral study would be if the organism under study was out of its natural environment. The kids had also started thinking about how to design an experiment to test the sensitivity of the worm to its environment. More specifically, the class was beginning to ask questions such as: Does an animal feel pain? How could this pain be measured?

It is important to note that the class was only just beginning to recognize the importance of taking accurate measurements of the animals' movements. Observations such as "All of a sudden, the worm has gotten very long" or "It moves rapidly" were not criticized by the class until two weeks later, when they undertook the class projects. It was only then that the kids began to quantify behavior. Still, they had already made a lot of progress.

PRODUCING EVIDENCE

The next phase of the earthworm work proceeded from the following assignment:

> Find out all the ways your worm is sensitive to the environment.

Rather than discussing ethical issues or behavioral research techniques, I wanted to stress scientific methodology. I wanted the kids to conduct a research project in the classroom, so I pushed them to explore the meaning of "sensitivity" in an earthworm. It was important for them to substantiate (with evidence) any conclusions that they drew.

The class was slower to get started on this assignment than they had been on the two previous exercises. They found this exercise more difficult than the others had been. However, they did finally come up with 12 different observations of worm responses to stimuli. They listed 7 behaviors that were responses to tactile stimuli, 4 to a chemical stimulus (water) and 1 to a visual stimulus (light from a flashlight).

How our worm responded to stimuli in its environment:

1. When touched by a probe, it flattens.
2. When sprayed with water, it curls up.
3. It avoids contact.
4. It moves away from light.
5. It moves into one of the corners.
6. It moves more rapidly in water.
7. It does not stay in a corner – it moves around the surface of the pan.
8. It tried getting out of a jar of water.
9. It moves faster in drops of water in the pan.
10. It cannot survive in 20ml of water.
11. It coils around a pin or pointed instrument.
12. It slips through the hole of a scissors handle.

I wasn't sure how to process this list. I noticed that there was one contradiction (i.e., the worm moves into one corner according to observation number 5, whereas in number 7, it does not stay in a corner). I began by asking for the reasons behind this inconsistency in the record. The ensuing discussion merely involved summary (rather than analysis) of their results, so little progress was made until Richie asked, "Are these worms really intelligent?"

I realized that this question could give direction to this class's inquiry. Instead of answering Richie's question outright, I asked him why that question had occurred to him. He said he had noticed that the worm always went to the same corner. He wanted to know if this was instinct or if the worm "knew" where it was going.

DESIGNING RESEARCH Richie's question led directly to the next small-group assignment:

Try to get your worm to go to the same corner of the pan.

This was the most difficult task so far, because they were now testing a hypothesis through experimentation. Some of the groups just suggested ways of testing the hypothesis, while other groups actually tried to do an experiment. All groups handed in some written work by the end of the period. The next day, I handed out copies of each group's work. I used one group's write-up to start the discussion for the following day's lesson:

Group members	Mike	**Materials**	Grass
	Ismael		Poison—not too strong
	Suzie		Water
			Flashlight
			Soil

Procedure

We put him in the middle of the tray, with 10% vinegar in one corner, water in another corner, grass in another, and the flashlight in the fourth corner. We tried to push him in the vinegar and he pushed away. We put him in the light and he looked like he was weak. We put him back in the middle and he went to the soil. We put 10% vinegar on the worm and then we put him in the 20ml of water. Then he died and his skin looked all baggy.

On the following day, I asked what problems they had encountered while testing the corner hypothesis. The students responded with statements like, "The worms died. They didn't go where we wanted them to. They were stupid." I distributed copies of Mike, Ismael, and Suzie's write-up to the class. The class's attention was thus focused upon that group's methodology and experimental design. Mike, Ismael, and Suzie were then encouraged to explain verbally their rather vague written work. The class asked them questions such as, "Why did you start in the center?" and "Why did you use soil, water, vinegar and light?" These questions forced the group to explain their procedures. The questions also gave rise to an array of thoughtful, related inquiries from the students:

Is a "reward" (grass or soil) more effective than a "punishment" (vinegar or light)? (Another group had suggested using electricity or heat as punishment.)

When is the best time to introduce the stimulus—before or after the worm gets to the corner?

How many times do you have to conduct the same experiment?

Can the worm smell the vinegar? How would his affect the experiment?

Does every corner have to have something different?

It was obvious that the class had begun to think more explicitly about the scientific process. The students were now critiquing each other's work and asking questions without prompting them.

I felt the class was now ready to be pushed to quantify. I asked the kids what a scientist needed to know about a chemical such as vinegar before presenting it as a stimulus. The class responded that the experimenter should know how much vinegar to use, how strong the vinegar should be, how much time to leave a stimulus in a corner before changing it, and whether the worm's movement to a particular corner even meant that the worm was intelligent. These prerequisites for investigation led to a discussion about conditioning and training; someone then raised the question of whether trainability implied intelligence.

I asked the class to think for a minute about how they would redesign Ismael, Suzie, and Mike's experiment. After a short discussion, the class decided that three corners should be the same, with only the fourth corner different, a much better controlled experiment. This is where the discussion ended, however. None of the questions the students had raised were answered or even discussed during the class session. I have come to recognize this as an integral part of the inquiry lesson—often, more questions are raised than are answered.

The class worked on earthworms for five days. At the end of the fifth day, I asked the class what they thought was important in doing an experiment. I listed their responses on a board at the front of the room:

Experiments have to be repeated.
Experiments need a control.
Experiments need correct measurements.
Experiments need patience.

I kept this list of generalizations about experiments in front of the room for the rest of the semester. The students added to it as they felt was necessary.

We were now two weeks into the course. My students were talking to each other a lot more, and they were asking each other questions. My practice of quickly returning their written work to them was important because they could clearly see the need for revisions. Returning cumulative class work the next day was also essential so that we could together figure out how to proceed with the work. Our aim was not necessarily to resolve the issues but rather to probe them further. In this way, we continued to pursue our inquiries into animal behavior.

Guest Speaker

AS PROBLEM PRESENTER

The next set of Animal Behavior activities revolved around the input of our first guest speaker, Dr. Karyl Swartz from Lehman College's Psychology Department. Exposing students to "experts" is an integral component of the inquiry method; speakers visit the Animal Behavior class almost once a week throughout the semester. We sometimes go to the speaker's place of work, and sometimes the speakers come to us. I think it is very important for the first speaker to come within the first two weeks of the course. Each speaker must understand his or her role in the classroom.

These speakers were intended to make the kids think through research designs and improve their interviewing skills. Whenever possible, I explain to the speaker (in advance of the visit) what I am trying to accomplish. I ask him or her to give a bit of background information, just enough for the kids to understand what the speaker's research is about. Beyond that, I feel that the speaker should speak as little as possible. Instead of lecturing, Animal Behavior speakers are intended to present research problems, explore solutions to those problems with student input, and elicit hypotheses and appropriate research designs from the class.

Although most speakers agree that this sounds like a wonderful way to conduct a class, they are nonetheless prone to falling into the old role of speaker-as-lecturer. I got lucky with Dr. Swartz, however. Her topic of investigation was how infant monkeys recognize their mothers. She was very animated, showed interesting slides, and managed to present the kids with a lot of factual information without boring them. She engaged their attention by having a dialogue with them, asking thought-provoking questions, and then addressing the kids' own ideas.

> DR. SWARTZ: How does the baby recognize its mother?
>
> STUDENTS: By her scent? By her sound? By her actions? By her color? By her general appearance (amount/type of fur)?
>
> DR. SWARTZ: These are all very good hypotheses. In my study, I happened to choose to test vision as the baby's way of recognizing its mother. Now, if you assume the baby recognizes its mother by sight, then the next step is to ask what the baby looks at when it recognizes its mother by sight.

In this manner, Dr. Swartz led them further into her study. For example, she posed the following questions for the students to ponder:

> How does a baby learn to love its mother?
> How does it learn who its mother is?
> How does the mother learn to love the baby?

Dr. Swartz was nonjudgmental about the kids' suggestions. She just talked to them, which I think helped to demystify the work of the scientist. She gave the kids a lot of positive feedback as well. She also stopped to give them time to think after she asked each question, waiting through silent periods for their responses.

At one point, Dr. Swartz told the kids about one of the problems in her research:

> DR. SWARTZ: When does the baby recognize its mother and how? Can you think of a way I could find this out?
>
> Victor: Separate the babies from their mothers.
>
> DR. SWARTZ: That's exactly what I did! I needed a control, though. I wanted the monkeys to respond only to visual stimuli (not behavioral stimuli) of the mother. How could I eliminate adult behavior so that I could use a visual stimulus?

THOMAS: Show the babies pictures of adult monkeys.

DR. SWARTZ: That's just what we did next.

This class session at Lehman lasted almost two hours. One period would not have been sufficient for the kids to explore some of these ideas. Allotting time for slides made Dr. Swartz's presentation more varied and more interesting to the class. For the most part, the kids were actively taking part in the discussion. They asked Dr. Swartz all kinds of questions, from the purely factual to the speculative (e.g., "suppose you did this…?"). Some of the students did tune out periodically, but they subsequently regained interest and joined the discussion again.

The speaker became more and more excited as the session continued. She became more involved with the class, as they continued to ask questions of her. She told me afterwards that she hadn't known what to expect and that she was very pleasantly surprised. She asked me how the students had been chosen for the class and whether the Animal Behavior class was special in some way. It was clear that Dr. Swartz was very excited about what had taken place. Actually, because of her enthusiasm, I developed a speaker questionnaire (see the Notes, p. 94) to gauge the quality of student-speaker interactions.

ESTABLISHING CRITERIA

The next day, I distributed a transcript of the students' questions and Dr. Swartz's responses. We discussed why Dr. Swartz was a good speaker as well as why she seemed to be a good scientist. The class, after discussing the nature of science and scientists, added the following criteria to the list of generalizations about good science that they had already begun to develop:

A good scientist learns by making mistakes.

A good experiment doesn't result in a single answer to a question. It makes you ask new questions.

Women can be scientists.

The students also liked Dr. Swartz as a speaker. They concluded the following:

A good speaker . . .   knows his/her subject.

is not afraid to ask questions.

is honest.

listens to our suggestions.

is organized.

is excited about his/her topic.

gets the class involved.

In compiling this list, the students established criteria for what makes a speaker good. These criteria later enabled them to compare one speaker with another. We even began to rate speakers on a scale from one to ten, so that the class could readily see the process of setting standards.

On the last day of the course, we were joined by a speaker who was conducting research on roaches. She brought containers filled with huge roaches, and allowed the insects to crawl all over her, which both repulsed and captivated the students. She was quite animated, and she was getting the students involved in the discussion. In essence, she had all of the makings of a good speaker. Had she been the first speaker of the semester, the class probably would have been taken in by her. However, once the novelty had worn off and the class started to interview her in earnest, the students began to question how good a speaker she really was.

After the speaker left, the class debated how to rate her speaking ability. She presented "facts" without explaining the scientific work that had led to those conclusions. She simply told the students that they could "read about it." The class felt that she was being evasive. They wanted me to invite her back for a debate with another scientist who "really knew what he was talking about." They also wanted to visit her lab. Although the semester had come to a close, the students were already planning for further inquiry. (See Notes, p. 95, for a complete list of speakers used during the semester.)

Class Project

GERBILS

At about three weeks into the course, I generally have the class begin a class project that will last at least one week. In this class, I chose gerbils to be the subject animals for the class project, but I had not yet chosen a specific focus. Each group of three to four students received a gerbil. The students were to describe the animal and write questions about it. Most of the groups reported that gerbils were friendly, curious, intelligent, and fast.

I thought that the class might ultimately attempt to test the intelligence of the gerbils, but I decided that they first ought to work on an easier project. I asked each group to come up with a way to determine the speed of their gerbil. I chose this problem for several reasons: it involved fewer variables than the intelligence question would, and so would be easier to control; it involved math skills; it would take a relatively short period of time to complete; and it would be fun for the kids.

The students had only a few minutes to consider the speed problem. Most of the groups missed the point entirely. They suggested timing the gerbil from a starting point to some end point, without regard for rate of speed. For example, one group discovered that the gerbil would move from point A to point B in two seconds, but the kids still couldn't tell me how quickly the gerbil was moving. No one in the class knew the formula for finding rate of speed, though they did have a vague notion that it involved both time and the distance traveled. Some kids likened gerbil speed to a car moving at X miles per hour. I then gave them the formula, Rate x Time = Distance. The class decided that each group would need a track and a stopwatch. After further discussion, they added rulers (to measure distance) to their list of equipment needed. I told them to go ahead and set up the track as they saw fit.

The groups used books and scrap wood to construct different runways. The gerbils were then set loose on the tracks. The groups soon began loudly encouraging their own gerbils to "win." Someone suggested that we hold a Gerbil Olympics to see whose animal was the fastest. A visitor or a passerby might have gotten the impression that the class was just being noisy, or that they weren't learning anything. After all, the kids were out of their seats, walking around the room, cheering the gerbils on to victory. This observer would probably not see what I began to notice amid all the confusion: that they were becoming groups, and the whole tone of the class was definitely changing.

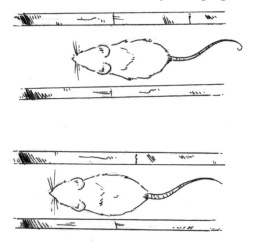

RATE X TIME = DISTANCE The next day, we discussed each group's results. The kids had trouble with the math, so together we calculated the rate with one group's data. The class then figured out the other groups' rates based on the data from the previous day. As I had suspected, each group arrived at a different rate of gerbil speed. We discussed the possible reasons for the discrepancies. The two fastest gerbils happened to be female, so the class felt that rate of speed might by sex-related. More generally, the students thought that differences in gerbil speed could stem from gerbil-to-gerbil differences in age, weight, condition, and sex.

We examined differences in speed-measuring techniques during class the next day. Everyone stood around each group's track while that group ran its experiment. Each group had to demonstrate how they had clocked the time and taken the measurements. With the whole class watching, they went through the experiment again. The students could then pinpoint sources of inaccuracy in the measurements taken. For example, the class noticed that even though some gerbils went backwards or moved from side to side down the track, several groups hadn't added that extra distance into their calculations. The kids thought that the track should be made smaller to prevent the gerbil from going backward or sideways. The class also concluded that a group should not stop timing a gerbil, even if it stopped moving. They then suggested that noise be eliminated because it appeared to distract the gerbils. Other criticisms raised by the class involved errors in math such as incorrect unit conversions, inaccurate timing, or incorrect division.

Through my nonjudgmental questioning (e.g., "What do you think about the way this group took their measurements?"), the class collectively came up with ways to improve their experimental designs. One group decided to take an average of three trials, which raised the question, "How many times do you conduct an experiment before you take an average?"

This short experience gave the class more practice to think about research design—the class began to consider more possible hypotheses to test and a wider range of variables to be controlled. The exercise can introduce the class to data collecting skills and it can act as an effective bridge to the larger project that follows. (See the Notes, p. 95, for a homework assignment on data collection.)

DETERMINING GERBIL INTELLIGENCE

The students were then ready to begin their first major class project. They were to devise experiments which would address the question, *How intelligent are gerbils?* I had several aims in designing this particular project. I wanted the kids to gradually become accustomed to staying with one task for longer and longer periods of time. Their final project would require working with a small group for about three weeks. This gerbil intelligence project would take one or two weeks, and so would "warm them up" for their final projects.

I also wanted to see how much the kids had learned from all the preceding mini-projects. I wondered whether their scientific thinking had sharpened as a result of trying to condition the earthworms or determine gerbil speed. Finally, I hoped that the class would continue to analyze how different groups approach the same task in different ways. Students would thus have additional opportunities to discuss the validity of particular techniques.

MAZES

The class decided to construct mazes and then try to determine how well the gerbils could learn the mazes. At first, the designs were fairly similar in that each one had only one entrance point and one exit point. The class also agreed that more complicated mazes would be better, that rewards (rather than punishments) should be given, and that food would probably be the best type of reward. In order to determine whether the gerbil had learned a maze, each group would time its gerbil and count the number of wrong turns the gerbil took each time it went through the maze. The groups had differed in terms of the number of false turns and dead ends the mazes had.

The class used cardboard folders to construct the mazes. Some groups began cutting and pasting immediately, designing the mazes as they went along. Other groups drew blueprints first, making changes on paper before beginning to build the maze.

My role during this time was simply to ask each group why they were constructing their maze the way they were, as well as what problems they expected

to encounter. Most groups wanted their mazes to be large, covering the surfaces of at least two student desktops. Some groups constructed mazes that were three or four feet on each side, with six or seven wrong exits. The rationale behind creating such a complicated maze was that the more complicated mazes could only be completed by more intelligent gerbils. I let the kids build upon their designs, despite the overwhelming difficulty of some of the mazes.

It was difficult for me not to interfere, particularly in the work of one group that had built very short walls for their maze. Gerbils are good climbers. The kids in that group told me not the worry, because their maze was "perfect." They soon discovered, however, that the gerbils could easily escape the maze. The group remedied the problem by covering the maze with a screen.

There was evidence that the groups were thinking through their experiments, trying in advance to eliminate variables that could influence their results. One group decided to do their project in an adjoining room in order to cut down on noise, which would be an added distraction. Another group covered all but the exit and the entrance points with plastic wrap in order to eliminate air currents.

The groups all began the actual testing on the same day. They ran the gerbils through the mazes for some time, and then we stopped to discuss results and problems. The students felt that their gerbils were stupid. Their evidence for this conclusion was as follows:

The gerbil did run through the maze, but never got to the exit. It kept making wrong turns.
The gerbil stayed in one particular part of the maze and refused to budge.
The gerbil did run through the first time, but it didn't eat the reward. It didn't find the exit the second time.

I asked the kids to think of reasons to explain these results. We discussed the following hypotheses and suggested remedies (in boldface):

1. The gerbils were not hungry enough, so the reward was meaningless. —**Withhold food.**
2. Regular gerbil food was not a sufficient reward.—**Offer special foods.**

3. The mazes were too complicated. —**Reduce the number of turns.**

4. Gerbils that didn't move were being distracted by people who were either tapping on the maze or else yelling at them to make them move. Gerbils in mazes set up on the floor were also distracted by the sight of the students that surrounded them.—**Raise the mazes up to eye level, stand back far enough to be out of a gerbil's field of vision, and don't tap or yell while the gerbils are in the mazes.**

One group complained that their gerbil hadn't moved, even though it wasn't being distracted by the students. That group had lined the correct path with food in order to encourage the gerbil, but it had stayed in one place to eat. Was this gerbil stupid, too? One kid suggested lining the correct path with cedar chips (instead of food) in order to accustom the gerbil to the maze. Another student critiqued this suggestion by pointing out that neither technique was good because neither one included controls. Both food and cedar chips added variables because they gave clues to the gerbil: "How do you know the gerbil isn't smelling his way out?" Someone then suggested that lining all of the paths (not just the correct one) with cedar chips would eliminate the added variable. Ultimately, the group decided to put nothing in the maze. It is important to emphasize that all of the above suggestions were offered by the students, not by me.

In order to make the gerbils hungry, which in turn would encourage them to seek food, the class decided to withhold food, but not water, for two days. Each group then wanted to retest the gerbil that they had tested the first day. The kids thus had to decide how they could identify each gerbil. Students suggested tying strings around each tail or otherwise marking each gerbil so that it couldn't lick off the marking. The class decided to mark the tails with a pen since strings would probably fall off and gerbils can't lick their tails. The students didn't account for the fact that gerbils lick each other's tails. Luckily, only two markings had been licked off by the end of the two-day fast.

The second maze experiment went much more smoothly than the first one had gone. In order to eliminate noise distractions, the groups dispersed throughout the room and the adjoining lab stockroom. This time, all of the animals went through the maze. Each group ran the experiment four or five times, and everyone collected data, although each group chose to do it differently. Some groups, for example, timed the animal (measured elapsed time), while others counted the number of wrong turns the gerbil made before finishing the maze.

The next day, we examined the results and discovered that, for three groups, the data showed no pattern or correlation. For each of these groups, the data varied widely between runs of the same maze. For two of the groups, however, a pattern was discernable: elapsed time decreased (the gerbils took less time to complete the maze), a trend that might indicate the gerbils were trainable. The data gathered by the sixth group remained consistent from the first to the fifth running of the maze.

The class tried to think of reasons why the results varied so greatly. After critiquing each other's experiments, they arrived at a consensus: the more complicated mazes yielded inconsistent data, while the less complicated mazes yielded data that would indicate gerbils are trainable. As often happens in an inquiry class, we raised more questions than we answered:

What makes a good maze?
If a gerbil runs through the maze, does that necessarily mean the gerbil is intelligent?
What is intelligence?
If the gerbil "learned" the maze, then what is learning?
What is the best way to illustrate data (charts, graphs, etc.)?
If we had more time, what else could be done with gerbils and mazes?

There were two significant changes during this project. Students played a much more active role critiquing each other's initial mazes. They listened more to suggestions and were more receptive to making changes. This was the least teacher-centered class experience thus far. The students also gathered more data than before. Their charting and graphing skills improved. They spent the most time discussing their data—not only the interpretation but also how the data were derived.

(See the Notes, p. 97, for a test evaluating the maze experience.)

5   Discussion of Project Designs

We next began to discuss different ideas for group projects. The whole class sat in a circle as each of the six groups explained what they were planning to do. There were three students per group. Each trio had thought about how to design their project, even though they had not yet written a project proposal. This class discussion was their first opportunity to really explore their project design ideas, though.

Many positive things came out of the discussion. The kids asked each other the types of questions that I had been asking them thus far. In addition, some useful suggestions were made to groups that were confused as to how to proceed. The discussion lasted an entire hour, and I rarely interrupted. This was the first time I saw the effects of inquiry on this class as a coherent group. The students listened to each other, they followed through on each other's questions, they were orderly. They were really conducting mature, professional interviews of each other.

One student, Suzie, had gotten back to a question that had given the class difficulty on the second day of the semester: "Do gerbils distinguish color?" She explained her group's design to the class: "Set up two doors, one green and one red. If the gerbil goes to the green side, reward it with food hidden behind that door. If it goes to the red door, give it a punishment, such as a shock or a smack with a ruler. We could also punish the gerbils by turning the light off." I asked the class if they had any comments on her group's design.

YVONNE: How do you know if the gerbil is responding to the color or to the smell of food?

SUZIE: Instead of food, I could use light. If it goes to the green door, I could put a light on, and if it goes to the red door, I could turn off the light.

VICTOR: But rats like the dark, so maybe gerbils like the dark too.

THOMAS: Also, how do you know it isn't going to the green door because it likes that side?

CARLTON: Maybe you should add another door. You could have two red doors and one green door.

RAY: Yeah, and then you could switch the green door around.

I used this little piece from the general discussion because I think it represents some very important changes that usually happen at this point in the course. First of all, in this class, the kids were critiquing on their own. They maintained this discussion throughout the entire period. I think it was a major step toward their becoming independent thinkers. They also were very respectful of each other; they listened to one another and the critiquing was solely of their research designs—not personal. Second, the above conversation shows that they were trying to get Suzie to think through her ideas by focusing on the variables in her rather vague design and how to eliminate or control them. Victor was, in effect, identifying assumptions that Suzie was making, that darkness was a form of punishment for gerbils and that gerbil punishments were the same as human punishments.

I think comparing this discussion with the response to the same gerbil color perception question much earlier in the term will give the reader a pretty good idea of the changes a class may make during the first month or so of the course.

Guest Speaker
AS CRITIC

Earlier in this course, a guest speaker, Dr. Swartz, helped the students to refine their thinking by talking with them about various ways of approaching a particular problem. Later, I used a speaker in a slightly different way. Since the kids had already begun working on their group projects, I invited another animal behavior teacher, Rudy Reiblein, to critique their projects and designs. An "outsider" often pushes the kids to think and to obtain information independently (i.e., without relying on their teacher). The "expert" also contributes an air of seriousness to the classroom.

I explained to Mr. Reiblein that I wanted him to simply ask the kids why they were carrying out the various projects in their particular ways. I hoped he would make them think about refining their designs. He proceeded to do this, focusing on each group in turn, and getting the whole class involved in each group's research. For example, this speaker got Suzie and her group to think further about their project on gerbil color discrimination.

SUZIE: Our project is "Do gerbils distinguish colors?"

MR. REIBLEIN: Nice project—clear goal. How are you setting up this experiment?

Suzie described how her group was using two boxes, one green and one red, each with a door cut out. Food was always placed behind the green door, but the gerbil had consistently gone through the red door.

MR. R.: What might be some of the problems with this set-up?

SUZIE: The gerbil might like the position of the red box instead of the color red. But that's the only problem I see. The gerbil just sees the door and goes in.

MR. R.: Why?

LORIE: The gerbils are curious.

MR. R.: What kinds of things do gerbils pay attention to?

CARLTON: People.

COOKIE: Noise.

MR. R.: So what do you have to do?

MANNY: Eliminate them.

MR. R.: Or standardize them. It could also be the light in the room. You should have the boxes in the same amount of light, with the same amount of vibrations on each side. Where are you standing?

SUZIE: In front.

MR. R.: What do you think about where Suzie is standing?

THOMAS: Maybe she's having an effect on the gerbils.

MR. R.: So what could she do?

LORIE: Step back.

VICTOR: Or put something in front of her.

MR. R.: Yes. That's called a blind. It eliminates extraneous stimuli. It could be just a piece of paper.

At the end of the hour, Mr. Reiblein told me that he hadn't known what to expect since he had never done anything like this before. After learning that this was a beginning science course, he was surprised to note that the kids had clear questions and that their projects were relevant, with appropriate controls. Speakers commonly comment that the nature and quality of the class's work surprise them. Despite the problems and frustrations I experienced with this particular class, in the end, I too was pleased and surprised by the extent to which the individual students, and the class as a whole, had evolved.

Another indication of this class's (the class I have been primarily discussing) growth in interviewing skills occurred towards the end of the semester, when the students were again interviewing the roach expert. Five or six teachers and supervisors who were observing the class felt compelled to ask questions themselves during the moments of silence when the kids were thinking of questions. One teacher whispered her question to one of the students, hoping that the student would ask it. When we discussed the interview the following day, the class felt that it hadn't gone as well as some of their previous interviews, because the visitors had "thrown off their rhythm." They hadn't been given the necessary time to think. It's important to tell visitors whose sole purpose is it observe the class that they must do only that.

SHARPENING INTERVIEWING SKILLS

I cannot over-emphasize the importance of guest speakers to the success of this course. For example, students in another Animal Behavior class offered several semesters later sharpened their interviewing skills tremendously through a series of interactions with guest speakers. When the first guest speaker of the semester, Captain Haggerty, director of a dog-training school, and his trained retriever, Ragamuffin, visited the class, only two or three kids asked questions. Captain Haggerty had to force each kid to ask him at least one question.

As the kids gained more experience, they became more and more confident interviewers. One day well into that semester I think they reached their peak. I expected each group to explain its experimental design to the guest speaker. I thought the groups would then critique one another's work. But this never happened. Instead, the class spent 45 minutes questioning a guest herpetologist who had brought in his 4-foot pet snake. I then became the "recording secretary." I didn't have to interrupt the process once. The students were self-propelled, initiating the interview themselves and sustaining the lesson on their own energy. They also raised several issues that gave direction to the class for the rest of the semester. The class period normally lasted fifty-five minutes, but in this case, the discussion continued for seventy minutes. The students were still asking questions, and they didn't want to leave. I had never before felt so positive about an individual class experience.

Role of the Inquiry Teacher

My role, at least in the beginning, is to establish an atmosphere in which students can feel comfortable about thinking through problems. I don't directly provide the students with answers; I instead try to respond to their questions and suggestions in ways that are non-judgmental and non-threatening yet will stimulate students to use their native talents to solve problems for themselves. Each student or small group of students is encouraged to work on a particular problem, using whatever style is comfortable or natural at that point in the course. This approach differs from the traditional student-teacher dynamic of the "developmental lesson" classroom. In a developmental lesson format, the teacher is usually the source of all the energy and most of the information in the classroom.

In an inquiry classroom, the teacher uses student energy to propel the class and to give it direction. The inquiry teacher thus becomes a facilitator. As the semester progresses, my role becomes less and less significant as the students, on their own, begin to apply techniques that I have used: asking each other "why?" and assessing each other's work.

Throughout the semester, I provide problems to be solved. I periodically invite guest speakers, who further stimulate student thinking in various ways. I also arrange trips on which students are asked to evaluate issues. Eventually, I am able to use class output (observations and experimental designs) as starting points for further research.

The course generally has the most dramatic impact upon students with ˙ reading and writing skills. (See the Notes, p. 97, for an example of a student˙ report.) Students who, for whatever reason, do not usually volunteer to class are also strongly affected by the course. In the case of the class I have been discussing, several students underwent especially remarkable changes in their behavior:

A student with very weak writing skills who rarely did homework for any class started to submit logs about his project and also submitted a fully-completed take-home final exam.

A very quiet student who initially did not volunteer to speak in class began to participate in interviews and also started to ask highly reflective questions. This student also participated in a discussion on the last day of class in which the students evaluated the merits of the final guest speaker.

Another quiet student began to critique a classmate's experimental design by asking, "But how do you know this?"

Another quiet student suddenly left the room to obtain a short interview from another teacher while the class was beginning to introduce the idea of a survey on snakes. This student, in her self-evaluation at the end of the semester, commented that she felt she had changed in her ability to ask questions of people she didn't know.

Under his own initiative, one student, telephoned the Director of the Animal Labs at Montefiore Hospital in order to request several rats for a maze he was building at home. The director subsequently gave him the rats, and the student submitted a written report of his independent work.

Another student voluntarily submitted an extra report for a project about ant communication that he had studied in his grandmother's backyard.

8   Issues to Think About

PROBLEMS

One of the biggest problems I tend to have is getting students to produce high-quality writing about their projects. There are several reasons for this difficulty. Many students think that writing science project reports will require special "scientific" or "technical" language. They perceive such writing as being different from (and more difficult than) "creative" writing. Students also feel that a scientific project report must be about a "completed" experiment. Kids sometimes complain that since "nothing happened," they have nothing to write about. Sometimes they find that what happened is very different from what they had anticipated. I have to explain that their writing should represent work-in-progress rather than finalized results.

Another problem that might emerge is that many of the students fail to submit homework regularly. I sometimes discuss this with my classes, and it seems that even though they feel the homework assignments are relevant (i.e., the students themselves have generated the ideas for the homework), the assignments are nonetheless unimportant to them. Other facets of their lives take precedence over doing the work.

SOME SOLUTIONS

In order to help students write their project progress reports, I have them start writing early in the course, and I explain that their work will ultimately be published in a booklet. I also invite "outsiders" to visit the class and give feedback on works-in-progress. For example, I recently had three college students, former students of mine, ask the current students questions about their work:

What was the question you were trying to answer or investigate?
How did you go about it?
Why did you proceed that way?
Did you encounter any problems?
How did you try to solve the problems that arose?
What were your results?
What conclusions did you reach?
What evidence do you have to support your conclusions?

This line of questioning helped the groups to start their final reports by making them think about what they had done. The college students took notes as the group answered the above questions. The notes were then given to the group to use in writing up their reports. Almost anyone who can listen and take notes can be used to facilitate this experience.

I also have developed a pre- and post- "test" for the Animal Behavior course that helps me assess how much the kids can do when they enter the course compared with what they know by the end of the term. (See the Notes, p. 99, for the pre-tests and p. 97 for an example of a post-test.) I have also sometimes presented the same mini-problem to the class during the first and last weeks of the course as another way of measuring their growth.

READING WRITING AND DEBATING

Over the years, I have developed a selection of non-fiction readings in animal behavior that has had wide appeal among my students and a number of strategies for teaching writing in the sciences. See the Notes section, beginning on p. 99, for more information and suggestions.

Conclusion

I have many surprises during each semester. For example, kids often remain beyond the fifty-five minute class period. If I don't dismiss the class on certain occasions, the students will never leave the room. Guest speakers want to know whether the students in the class are special and how they have been chosen for the class. One speaker, a teaching assistant from Albert Einstein University, once remarked that the class conducted a better interview than some college classes she had visited.

My own reaction to the inquiry class is perhaps the greatest surprise. Throughout the term, I generally experience a very wide range of emotions—from deepest frustration and pain (near the beginning of the course) to extremely positive feelings later on. It is exhilarating to see that a course that emphasizes scientific process can be successful. The inquiry course is much more valuable, both to me and to my students, than a course with a traditionally prescribed curriculum would be. I'm constantly questioning my own established pattern of teaching, and asking myself, Why am I doing this? Is there another way to present this information to students, such that their thinking is stimulated and their latent abilities to solve problems are tapped?

NOTES

CHAPTER 1

ESTABLISHING AN ATMOSPHERE

LIST OF 92 QUESTIONS, Week 1

Gerbils

How long does it take for baby gerbils to grow hair?

How long does the female carry her babies?

How do all the babies fit inside a little gerbil?

Why does the parent make holes and then put the babies in them?

Will the parents kill the babies if you touch them?

What kind of food does the gerbil eat?

How can you tell the male from the female?

Does the cold have an effect on gerbils?

How long does it take for baby gerbils to open their eyes?

Why are their eyes closed for so long?

What's the difference between hamsters and gerbils?

How does the mother know which is her baby?

What's the difference between a gerbil and a mouse?

What happens to a gerbil when it is out of its cage?

How old are they?

What colors can they see?

How big are they going to get?

Why do they like to chew on the paper tube?

How many babies do they have at one time?

How long does it take for them to stop being fed by their mothers?

How many babies can a gerbil have at a time?

Hooded Rats

Why are they called hooded rats?
Do hooded rats come from the same family as the regular rats?
How do hooded rats reproduce?
Will they get any bigger?
Do they bite?
Do hooded rats only come in two colors?
Why do they have big feet?
Are they very friendly when they get to know you?
Do hooded rats eat any food?

Garter Snakes

How long does a garter snake grow?
How many years does a snake live?
How many babies does it have?
How many times does it shed?
How can you tell which sex is which?
Does a snake like to be alone when it sheds its skin?
What does it like to eat?
Why does it remove its skin?
How do they move so well without feet?

Chameleons

How large does the chameleon grow?
Why do they change color?
How much and what do they eat each day?
Do lizards use their tails for anything special?
How long does it take for the color to change?
I thought chameleon's eyes were circular and bulge outwards—I don't think they
    are.
Can a lizard survive in all types of weather?
If a lizard's tail breaks off, would it grow two?
How many eggs can they (re) produce at a time?

Hamsters

How old is she?
Do hamsters get along with gerbils?
Why do hamsters like lettuce?
Why is she so mean?
Is there a specific reason why she killed her mate/son?
What is their life span?

Fish

How do they reproduce?
How many different kinds of fish are in the world?
How many babies do they have?
What happens if you mix different kinds of fish together?
Why do they jump like they are always scared when you hit the glass?
Why doesn't the fish blink its eyes?
Why is that orange fish's skin clear?
How long can they live without food?
Why are they so thin?
Why are they so secretive and don't rest?
Why are they named "kissing" fish?
Why do the fish seem to follow each other?

Frogs

Why does a frog stay still for such a long time?
How many eggs does a frog lay?
Why do they like to jump around so much?
How do the males court the females?
What do frogs like to eat, other than flies?
How does the frog cause people to get warts?
Do they ever go to sleep?
What purpose do they serve?

Earthworms

Why does it go down to the bottom when I bring it to the top?
When you try to touch them, they run away quickly.

What do you feed them?
How big do they get?
Why do they live in dirt?
How can they survive in the dirt?
Why are these worms called earthworms?
Are earthworms similar to leeches?
How do they get that reddish color?
How does the earth (or land) benefit from them?

Ants

How do ants reproduce?
How can they pick up the grains of sand?
Are all these ants workers?
What does the ant like to eat?
How big do ants grow?
For ants to be so small, how come they are so strong?
Why do ants build tunnels?
Can ants form communities?

CHAPTER 3   **GUEST SPEAKER AS PROBLEM PRESENTER**

SPEAKER EVALUATION FORM

We are interested in how you, the speaker, felt about your visit. Would you please answer the questions below in as much detail as possible. (Use the reverse side, if necessary.) Thanks very much.

How would you compare this group to others you've had experience with?
Please comment on the types of questions that were asked (content, knowledge, phrasing, etc.)
Which questions were specifically significant in some way to you? Please explain why.
Did anything happen during this class that you found unusual or unexpected? Please explain.

Please comment on the role you played today. (Did you feel or do anything differently?)

Please comment on the strengths and weaknesses of this group.

What is your impression of the academic level of the group? (above average/average/below, etc.)

What recommendations would you make to the group for when the next speaker comes?

General comments or questions you have. (Please use the reverse side.)

SPEAKERS AND TRIPS DURING ONE SEMESTER

Professor/researcher, Psychology Dept., Lehman College

Professor, Biology Dept., Hostos Community College

Roach behaviorist, American Museum of Natural History

Animal behaviorist, Animal Medical Center (trip)

Teaching assistant, Simian Aides, (using monkeys with paraplegics), Albert Einstein Medical College

Professor, Psychology Dept., Fordham University

Biology teacher, independent high school

Director of dog training school (with dog)

Doctor/Director, Animal Care, Montefiore Hospital (trip)

Assistant Professor of Biology, Lehman College

Teaching assistant, Albert Einstein Medical College (returns with monkey)

The Bronx Zoo (trip)

Student with 4-foot pet snake

Roach behaviorist, American Museum of Natural History (returns)

CHAPTER 4   CLASS PROJECTS: GERBILS

HOMEWORK ASSIGNMENT

Observe the behavior of an animal (or an infant) for three days. Write down your observations.

The object of this assignment is to get students to see the importance of writing a good observation. I type them all and give each group a packet of observations and ask them to choose which is the best and explain why. In so doing, they are establishing criteria for a good observation, without necessarily using any of the formal "technical" language.

I chose this student's work to reproduce because, as the class pointed out, Ismael did three very important things:

Timed the animal (sense of numbers)
Told the story of what happened (sequence of behavior)
Counted how many times (frequency details)

Ismael Castro
I have two pigeons I observed for 5 minutes the day of Feb. 7. To observe them you have to be very quiet because they are very shy. For 2 minutes the male bugged at the female. (Bugging means showing and telling her he's in control there.) The female stood in the corner jerking her wing, making a noise to her mate, bringing her head up and down as she moaned. The next couple of minutes the male ate food from the cage such as corn and grip.

Next day, Feb. 8, about the same time. The male was bugging at the female again but this time she was walking around the cage. He walks around her giving her the love sign, which is going around her throwing his body into hers, pushing her to a corner from the bottom up. Then when she's ready she will put out her beak. Then he will grab it. Then they start kissing.

The last day, Feb. 9. They went and did almost the same thing as the day before, except they had SEXUAL INTERCOURSE. They do it twice, sometimes three times. The first time it takes 2 or 3 seconds. The second time it takes about 4 seconds. First they kiss about 3 times. Then when the female is ready, she gets down until her chest touches the floor. Then the male jumps on top of her, putting his tail under hers, flapping his wings so that he won't fall. Sometimes she opens her wings so that she won't fall sideways. After 4 seconds it's over.

CLASS TEST

This test is given after the class has built their own mazes.

General Directions

1. Answer all questions on a separate sheet of paper.
2. Answer as completely as possible. Use as many details as possible.
3. The questions are based on the maze that you see in front of you.

Questions

1. A gerbil will go through the maze during the next five minutes. Record all of your observations of the gerbil in the maze.
2. a) Is this a good maze for a gerbil to learn? Answer this question giving as many specific and detailed reasons as possible to support your answer.
   b) Give this maze a grade (from 0-100%)
3. List all of the ways you would improve this maze. Make a separate list of the best ways to carry out the experiment. Explain why each suggestion is on your lists.

CHAPTER 7 **ROLE OF THE INQUIRY TEACHER**

FINAL PROJECT

It's very important to keep in mind that the following example of a student final report is a work in progress and not a final paper. The paper was a first draft, written at the end of the term when there was not time for any revisions.

It was written by a student with reading and writing skills below grade level. Although I would question the reward system, I think the paper shows tremendous growth in the ability to think through a problem because the student:

- Clearly defines the problem
- Accurately discerns the differences between experimental and control components of the experiment
- Suggests two different logical interpretations of the results

- Describes two valid ways to redesign the experiment based upon these interpretations
- Avoids making any definitive conclusions (possibly because of lack of supporting evidence)

Sample Student Report

I started the project by looking through books about animals and experiments, after looking through I decided to choose the rat because I like rats and they are very interesting to work with.

The question I am trying to answer is, Can a rat identify a design?

The way I set up my experiment was I took a box and put three doors in it, and then I drew two designs in two of the doors the same and the third door was different, then I surrounded the box with wood so the rat would not escape.

Now I have three doors cut out, in the box two of the doors are the control, they are the same, the third door is a different design which is the experimental.

When I first put the rat in the box, the rat was not used to it, it was very very nervous, and was always trying to get out, so I put in a younger rat, this rat was more active, and curious.

I used the same rat again and I put food in the middle door and the rat would go in.

Three out of five times the rat went through the middle door which is the experimental.

What I think is that the rat went through the middle door because there was food behind the door that I put there, and not because of the design. So the next day I did not put any food at all in none of the doors, and the rat went in through the middle door. I think the rat went in the middle door because of his own scent that he was there before and he can sense the food was there before but not because of the design on the door.

The way I controlled my experiment is by cleaning out my set-up each time after the animal has been inside. I also limit the noise.

If I had more time I would have switched the design to the other side and see what would happen, then I would have changed it back to the way it was.

PRE-TESTS

Test A

(Drawing taken from The Tree Puzzle, Knott, Lawson, Karplus Their & Montgomery, 1978)

Imagine you take a walk in a park and see these two trees with the grass below them. Does what you see raise any questions?

If yes, what question(s) is raised?

What might be some answers to this question?

Pick one of those answers and describe an experiment to find out whether the answer is correct or not.

Test B

How do infant monkeys recognize their mother?

This is one question that infant behaviorists are trying to answer.

What do you think might be the possible answers to this question? (Use the other side if necessary.) Your possible answers to the question are known as hypotheses.

Choose one of your possible answers mentioned above. Describe how you would conduct an experiment that would test this hypothesis. (Use the other side if necessary.) Please describe your experiment in as much detail as you can.

List five problems you might face while conducting this experiment. What do you think you might do to try to solve each of them? (Use the other side if necessary.)

SUGGESTED READINGS

I want the kids in my class to get more experience reading works of nonfiction. I often bring in articles from *Discover* or *Natural History* magazines. These readings give the kids an opportunity to learn how experts record animal behavior. The kids are then able to compare the scientific methodologies of the studies they read about. I have also tried giving students original-source articles from scientific journals (found in the American Museum of Natural History's library, for example) on topics related to their own. The group then discusses the evidence cited in the research as well as the conclusions drawn about an animal's behavior. The classroom library, which includes both popular and professional scientific literature, has become a valuable resource for the Animal Behavior class.

Another way to incorporate more readings, is to have each student read at least one book that deals with the behavior of a particular animal or a book that contains a collection of animal behavior essays. Because of the heterogeneous classes I teach (reading skills, ages, cultural backgrounds), I need to supply the class with a wide range of books. Some of the books that have been selected by students are:

A Cat is Watching, by Roger A. Caras
Adam's Task, by Vicki Hearne
Born Free, by Joy Adamson
Gorillas in the Mist, by Dian Fossey
In the Shadow of Man, by Jane Goodall
Lads Before the Wind, by Karen Pryor
Never Cry Wolf, by Farley Mowat
Unnatural Acts, by David Quannam

I require each student to submit at least one book report. The following is the formal assignment:

How Well Does Your Book Discuss the Behavior of an Animal?

Maximum—750 Words

I. Choose any two chapters that you feel best discusses the behavior of an animal. For each chapter:

A. Clearly state at least three reasons why you think it best discusses the animal's behavior.
B. Include a discussion of the evidence found in the chapter that supports each of your reasons. Include the best examples of evidence. You may use brief quotes from your book. (Three sentences maximum for each quote.)

II. Choose the one chapter that you feel has the worst discussion of the animal's behavior.
   A. Clearly state at least three reasons why you think the author was not so successful in discussing the animal's behavior in this chapter.
   B. Include a discussion of the evidence. (Follow the same guidelines as for I.B. above.)
III. Choose any conclusion that the author reached about the animal's behavior (from anywhere in your book).
   A. What did the author find out about the animal's behavior?
   B. Discuss how the author reached this conclusion. (What did the author or the scientists do? What was the evidence on which the conclusion was reached?)
IV. Write a recommendation of this book that you would make to a friend. Clearly explain, using examples from the book (be brief), why you are making this recommendation.

The book report is introduced within the first two weeks of the semester. This allows the students the chance to experience some of the inquiry-type activities that were discussed in the beginning, and also gives them ample time to read and complete the written assignment.

I have arrived at this particular book report format for a variety of reasons. I decided to give the students a maximum word limit, instead of the usual minimum, so that they are forced to express themselves as succinctly as possible. The specific book report question was chosen because I didn't want the report to be a mere summary of the book. I wanted the students to be more reflective about what they read.

Since most kids have little or no experience reading works of nonfiction (which requires different skills from reading novels), I developed the book report guidelines to help students know how to read the book and what to look for. This is why I especially included the search for evidence.

The book report format purposely included choices. I have found that this helps students to not become intimidated by fairly lengthy or technical books (like *Gorillas in the Mist*). It also forces the student who does read the entire book to make more reflective choices. The format can easily be modified to accommodate students reading collections of essays (like *Adam's Task*).

Along with the readings, I find myself making greater use of videotapes, particularly the series on animal behavior done by PBS. In this series, a problem is presented at the beginning of the program (e.g., "Can bees see certain colors?"). Once the question has been presented, I stop the tape and ask the class how they would design an experiment to address that question. I let them work in small groups. We reconvene to discuss their designs, and I then start the tape again so that they can see how the "experts" did it.

Another way I use video is to show a one-minute segment of taped animal behavior and then ask the class to make a list of everything they observed. A variation of this would be to turn off the sound and ask them to list any questions they might have about that animal's behavior.

BOOK REPORT—TEACHING STRATEGIES

At this point I think it would be very useful to describe a few teaching strategies connected with the book report.

After students give me a list of animals they would prefer to read about, the very next time the class meets I display all of the books (several with multiple copies). The kids then are given as much time as they wish to browse through the books. (I do, at this point, tell them that they need not necessarily have to read the entire book for the report to help encourage students to look through the thicker books.)

Once books are selected I have found it is important to make sure the kids are keeping up with the reading. One strategy that is useful here is to give the students very short progress reports to complete. The progress reports are given at regular intervals (for example, one every three class meetings). Usually after the fifth progress report the final book report is due.

The progress reports begin very traditionally and gradually include more questions that have to be thought through. For example, progress report number one might ask merely for the setting, any important events occurring thus far, and any additional student comments. A question on progress report number five might be: Choose a question about your animal that the scientist's work raises. Describe how you would design an experiment that could effectively investigate this question.

If students are unhappy with the book selected, they may make another selection after the first or second progress report. It is at this point that students are given the final book report format.

Another strategy I have found extremely useful is to have kids talk about the books that they are reading. I try to do this as often as possible. But since many different books are being read, it is important to plan activities that can involve anyone. One particularly effective activity is to have students select passages that will be shared with the whole class during the next meeting. The passages can be selected on any number of topics—for example, descriptions of "good" or "bad" animal observations, scientific work, or writing styles. Students have also chosen passages that they found unexpected or surprising in some way. These passages (usually no more than one page in length) are reproduced for the entire class in time for the next meeting. It is extremely important that the class examines at least two selections. This makes it possible for a greater exchange of different ideas, which can lead to more issues being raised for the class to analyze in the future.

RESEARCH PAPERS—TEACHING STRATEGIES

It would take another publication (at least!) to adequately describe this process. I'm constantly rethinking and refining the strategies that are needed to teach the writing of research papers. There are many skills that have to be taught and each one has it particular set of problems that have to be overcome. But I think that my attempts might be useful for teachers who are considering adding research paper writing to their classes.

The initial concept for writing papers came out of a class trip to the Central Park Zoo. (See p. 108 for the Zoo Assignment Sheet.) A lively discussion occurred during the class that followed the trip. Several issues about zoos were raised, including: Are zoos the best places for animals? What should be the function of a zoo? What do we learn about animals at the zoo? Varied opinions on each of these questions were expressed. It was clear that students disagreed with one another. One student boldly blurted out, "The Central Park Zoo should be closed down! We would all be better off if it did!" This last statement ignited even further disagreements which were becoming increasingly emotional (and less thoughtful) as the period drew to a close.

Afterward, I started to think about what had occurred during the class. On the surface it did appear that there was a very high degree of involvement. Some thoughtful issues were raised and students were freely defending their particular points of view. But looking back at the discussion, I realized how inadequately the students were thinking through their positions. One major problem was that they were not using evidence to support any of their arguments (which were filled with much misinformation). The kids needed to do research!

The following day I decided to have a debate in class about the main issue of whether or not zoos should exist. I think I may need to explain here why I chose this activity to initiate a research paper-writing project. Like the book report, the research paper is not meant to be an exercise in summarizing information. The research paper is another way in which students have to think through this information. (Of course, in the case of research papers there are additional skills involved, like the ability to organize the information gathered.)

To give you a better idea of what I was trying to do here, you need to see the research paper guidelines:

Write a Well-Organized Research Paper that Analyzes the Question: Should Zoos Continue to Exist?

In your research paper include:

Introduction: This is usually short—approximately one paragraph (five to six sentences). It should help the reader understand the question you will be analyzing. (It helps to write the introduction last, after you have done all of the necessary reading and writing.)

Discussion: This explains to the reader all of the different viewpoints people have on the main question, Should zoos continue to exist? You also have to explain why these people have their particular points of view. How did they arrive at their ideas? What is the evidence that supports their points of view?

Analysis: This part of your paper requires the most thought. Here you explain to the reader what you think about these different viewpoints, particularly what you think about the supporting evidence. You should discuss the strong and weak points of the evidence presented. Clearly explain your reasons for these judgments. For example, how would someone show the faults in the evidence that you think is weak? This is the part of your paper that I look at the most critically. It is the part that you will probably need the most help writing.

Conclusion: This part, like the introduction, need not be very lengthy. Write a concluding statement that can focus the reader on the problems involved in trying to find answers to the original question. In this part you may also mention what further questions have arisen that remain unanswered.

Bibliography: This is the list of sources (authors and titles) that you used.

Please note that this paper will be revised at least once.

As you can see, what distinguishes this paper from the typical "encyclopedic" type is the inclusion of the analysis section. This is why I decided to begin this writing project with the debate. I wanted the class to first hear the different points of view as well as the supporting arguments.

DEBATE AS BRIDGE TO WRITING

It can be a good idea to have experts (or available staff members) debate the issues so that the kids can hear new pieces of information that challenge their beliefs as well as subtler sides of issues that they have not yet considered. But, in one class, I did not have enough time to arrange this (as sometimes happens), so I planned to have a couple of student volunteers debate the issue. I decided that as the two students prepared their positions, the rest of the class would look at a news article related to the topic to help them compile a list of questions for the debaters.

But again, as sometimes happens, I did not carry out my original plans. Two students instantly volunteered to assume the pro and con position—that zoos should or should not continue to exist. They both assured me that they didn't need any preparation time—they already were familiar with their arguments. Without any prior planning, I instinctively told them that, since they were such knowledgeable experts, each of them would have to debate the side that they disagreed with. (The "pro" students would become the "con" student and vice versa). The job for the rest of the class was to take notes during the debate and prepare a list of questions for each of the debaters.

After a brief period of alternating protests and encouragement, the debate began. The format was as follows:

- each debater states a position with supporting evidence—five minutes for each debater
- debaters argue with one another—ten to fifteen minutes
- summations – two minutes for each debater
- members of the class ask the debaters questions – remainder of the period, less than five minutes

My role throughout the debate was only to facilitate the ordering of the class questions. I also took notes (which were distributed to the class when it next met). The homework assignment for the class was to evaluate the debaters, the class's questions, and list new questions that arose about zoos. The assignment for the two volunteers was similar except that each one had to describe the experience of taking on a position that the student disagreed with.

The debate was very effective. The two student volunteers said that arguing a point of view that they disagreed with was the hardest thing they had ever done. It was really tough to maintain their roles—to first have a clear idea of the counterpositions and then to think about the appropriate opposing arguments. To be honest, this was exactly the response I was hoping for.

The debate was extremely useful as a bridge to the writing project in other ways as well. The class was able to flush out some of the additional issues: What effect does a zoo have on an animal's behavior? Should zoos try to save endangered species? (This led to several crucial questions about the nature of evolution.) Would people learn more about an animal's behavior by watching nature programs on TV? How accurate are these programs?

The kids realized that they needed more information. For example, there were different opinions about how zoos affected the behaviors of particular animals—specifically monkeys, snakes, and bears. There were also contrasting opinions about the best way to construct habitats for certain types of animals (wolves, the entire cat family, as well as the monkeys, snakes, and bears).

For me, there was an even more significant outcome of the post-debate discussion. The kids also began to realize that the existence of zoos was not a simple "pro" –"con" issue. A couple of students said that they thought they knew "where they stood" but now they were beginning to get "confused." For example, on the species preservation issue, maybe zoos should not carry out this function. Maybe these animals are "naturally becoming extinct." Perhaps zoos should exist then only to educate the public. Several other students had different viewpoints. They felt that zoos should exist only to try to preserve endangered species, since "you can't learn anything about animals anyway at the zoo". Yet there was one student who insisted that "you can learn a lot about snakes just by watching them at the zoo."

As you can see, this is a good time for me to get the kids to begin the next phase of the research paper project.

My next step in the process is to give the kids a piece of reading to look at together in class. The essay chosen at that time was "Against Zoos" by Dale Jamieson, which appears in the collection *In Defense of Animals,* edited by Peter Singer.

I think it would be useful to briefly explain each of the remaining steps in this process, and then to discuss problems generally encountered and ways those problems can be avoided.

When the kids read the above-mentioned article, I had them highlight the important ideas. Then, each student held up the highlighted article, so that everyone else could see it. The class collectively highlighted almost everything! This led to a discussion about what was important and why.

I then distributed the research paper guidelines. I particularly concentrated discussing the analysis section, making connections with the outcomes of the debate. I then had the kids go back to one of the sections of the article we had read, asking them to come up with some arguments someone who disagreed with the article would have.

During the next class meeting, the kids developed a list of reasons why zoos should or should not exist, which I wrote on the chalkboard. (The list was actually just a summary of all of our previous discussions.) Then, on one of the tables in the classroom, I arranged piles of reading materials that corresponded to each of their anticipated items on the list. (Yes—this does require much work for the teacher; collecting and reading articles for different levels of reading, as well as having them all duplicated and collated.)

Their directions were to choose any article from any pile, begin to read it and highlight for viewpoints and evidence (and anything else they felt was important). Folders were distributed to everyone. Later each student selected articles to take home.

And so the research papers were begun.

This project is generally initiated about three-quarters of the way into the course, when students are also working on their individual animal behavior projects. I wanted the class to work on the research papers at home. However, if they were waiting for some equipment for their experiment to be delivered, or if a partner was absent, they could always work on their papers during class (extra copies of the articles were on file in the room). This not only provided some variety, but also prevented any student from ever saying that they "had nothing to do."

As with the book reports, I find it extremely useful to have periodic discussions about how the class is progressing with the papers. Also, I have learned from experience to give the class definite deadlines for submitting the different sections of the paper. In this way I am able to get completed papers (eventually!) from everyone.

The book reports provide for individual differences among students and so do the research papers. I provide a very large range of types of reading material—from daily newspaper articles to original papers published in scientific journals. Degree of student effort (and growth over the course of the semester) can then be evaluated in terms of quality and quantity of readings selected.

The two major problems that the students have are, not surprisingly, in organizing and analyzing their information.

As stated above, I find the debate to be extremely useful in this regard. I think it should ideally be immediately followed by a short piece of research writing. Perhaps writing a full research paper is sometimes too much of a leap for the kids. In terms of my particular course, the shorter piece of writing can be one of the questions that arise from the debate, for example, What affect does a zoo have on an animal's behavior? I think that all of the skills required for the full research paper definitely come into play here.

I also find that it is better to try to begin this project earlier in the semester, so that there is more time for individual conferences and revisions. Providing time for the sharing of student work with the rest of the class is very helpful as part of this revision process.

CENTRAL PARK ZOO ASSIGNMENT

***RETURN THE COMPLETED ASSIGNMENT TODAY WHEN THE TRIP IS OVER!

On a separate sheet (or sheets) of paper, respond to each of the following:

- Write a detailed observation report of any two different animals. Observe each one for at least ten minutes. The animals chosen must be from different habitats.
- List at least three questions that are raised by each of the observations.
- Choose any one question. Describe an experiment that would attempt to find possible answers to the question. Include all of the possible hypotheses and how you would test each of them.
- Name two animals that are best served by this zoo. For each animal, list at least five reasons to support your opinion.
- Name two animals that are least well served by this zoo. For each animal, list at least five reasons to support your opinion.
- Describe how you would change this zoo to better serve one of the animals you mentioned above. List at least five specific ways you would change the zoo.
- Any additional comments?

Produced at The Print Center, Inc. 225 Varick St., New York, NY 10014, a non-profit facility for literary and arts-related publications. (212) 206-8465